I0759570

Christ Before Caesar is a work of gravity and grace—a symphony of truth drawn from deep wells of Scripture, history, and confession. With precision and resolve, Thoma writes not to flatter the faithful but to awaken us, tracing with care the fault lines that divide courage from compromise. This is a call to allegiance—to the cross, and to the One who died upon it and who reigns over history. This is a clarion summons to the Church to remember who she is and whom she serves.

— Timothy Goeglein, vice president of external and government relations for Focus on the Family

Pastor Thoma provides a rundown of the challenges of our time with insightful reflections on how to address these matters head-on. This is not the descent into despair; this is a manual for Christian soldiers. Take up your arms—we have work to do! The gates of hell will not prevail against Christ's Church. Don the full armour of God and let us go on a crusade to restore Christendom. *Christ Before Caesar*! *Deus vult*!

— Father Calvin Robinson, UK political adviser, TV anchor, radio presenter, conservative commentator, and parish priest

Pastor Thoma's *Christ Before Caesar* is a sorely needed book at a time when the climate for truth-tellers in America is hostile and contradictory. A hyper-individualistic online culture encourages people to cling to vague moralism and personal opinion over religious confession. At the same time, political polarization means that many of the loudest voices are swayed by tribalism and groupthink without even realizing it. Thoma has carefully considered all the present problems of Christians engaging in the public square and offers solutions firmly rooted in careful historical analysis and solid Lutheran doctrine. He is especially good at articulating and defending Two Kingdoms theology and the benefits of religious liberty. *Christ Before Caesar* will no doubt inspire readers to speak eternal moral truths clearly and courageously.

— **Mollie Ziegler Hemingway, American conservative author, columnist, and political commentator**

CHRIST BEFORE CAESAR

CHRIST BEFORE CAESAR

Faithful Public Witness in an Age of Retreat

Christopher I. Thoma

FIDELIS PUBLISHING ®

ISBN: 9798999024619
ISBN (eBook): 9798999024626

Christ Before Caesar
Faithful Public Witness in an Age of Retreat

Cover Design by Diana Lawrence
Interior Design by Lisa Parnell
Edited by Amanda Varian

Order at www.faithfultext.com for a significant discount. Email info@fidelispublishing.com to inquire about bulk purchase discounts.

Fidelis Publishing, LLC • Winchester, VA / Nashville, TN
fidelispublishing.com

Manufactured in the United States of America

10 9 8 7 6 5 4 3 2 1

FIDELIS
PUBLISHING

For Charlie

Contents

Section 2

Section 3

Introduction

What My Daughter Brought Home from School

The times are changing quickly. In nearly every corner of American life, the Christian's public voice is being quieted. It doesn't always happen by force but often by misconception or fear, resulting in a willful withdrawal. That's the essential intersection of this book's examination.

That said, what follows is also meant to encourage. It is not just a call to clarity but to courage—to reclaim a faithful presence, and to reenter the public square not with hostility but with conviction. It begins, as many important things do, with a simple question brought home by a child.

Not long ago, my daughter received a two-sided page in her high school history class. Her teacher read the page aloud, presenting it as a historical analysis of early twentieth-century fascist regimes and a comprehensive definition of fascism. Wisely, my daughter asked for a copy of the document, which she brought home to share with me.

She questioned the information's legitimacy.

The page was excerpted from an article by Dr. Laurence Britt. A quick investigation led me to the article's original version on SecularHumanism.org. However, the page shared in my daughter's class was downloaded directly from Ratical.org, a site with an openly "progressive" editorial stance—thus, the site's name, a play on the word "radical."

Before reading any further, remember: While a teacher might usually provide hard copies of crucial course information that eventually ends up in the hands of parents helping their students to study, my daughter's teacher did not do so with this document. My daughter had to request it. That's suspicious. And yet, measured against Britt's concluding rhetorical sarcasm warning that fascism is being reborn in contemporary America, the teacher's goal comes more into focus.

The excerpted page presented a list of signs—fourteen in all—each lifted from Nazi Germany, fascist Italy, and others. As a concerned parent—and as a pastor trained to read texts with a critical eye—it was not difficult to see Britt's article is intellectually careless. He's historically imprecise, dangerously reductive at every turn, and leaves his bias against conservatism and Christianity hidden in plain sight. Right from the beginning, he refers his readers to the "Affirmations of Humanism" and then insists the affirmations are logically sound and crucial interpreters.

And yet, what follows is a political morality tale, with secular humanism as the hero and a thinly veiled caricature of conservatism and orthodox Christianity as the villains. Of course, he never directly names the targets of his critique. Instead, Britt's descriptors—catchy slogans, pride in the military, anti-abortion stances, religious devotion, patriotism, national security, homophobia, rigid traditional gender roles, and others—leave little room for doubting who he's describing.

Unsurprisingly, Britt does not expand the actual arguments or critique these positions objectively, but rather he simply inserts them into the fascist framework. The implication is therefore clear: Conservatism, nationalism, and Christianity are proto-fascist threats.

As a writer, I know rhetorical manipulation when I read it. Britt's words are not analytical. When presented to students as a definitive culmination of the subject, they become unfiltered indoctrination. It is a guilt-by-association argument designed to stigmatize conservative values by comparing them to the likes of Hitler and Mussolini without a sliver of actual evidence or balance. Even a little bit of either could have alleviated this sense. Instead, for example, Britt simply establishes national pride, concern for crime, support for police, and respect for the military as signs of creeping totalitarianism, even though they are natural to nearly every society, no matter its government or political structure.

But then his treatment of religion.

Britt explains how fascist regimes tend to align with a nation's predominant religious group to establish political dominance. He implies that in America, Christianity is the predominant religion, and therefore, Christianity's engagement in the public square is inherently fascistic. This is a gross oversimplification. While some twentieth-century fascist leaders paid lip service to religion, most were actively hostile to Christianity.[1] Hitler despised orthodox Christianity and sought to replace it with a racialized pagan nationalism.[2] Mussolini was a committed atheist.[3] To pretend fascism is inherently religious—or Christian engagement in the public square is a form of fascism—is, quite simply, historically ignorant.[4] Christians were among fascism's earliest and most consistent opponents.[5] Pastor Dietrich Bonhoeffer, who stood against Hitler and ultimately died for it, remains one of the most recognizable examples.[6]

Britt (and therefore my daughter's teacher) wants his readers to know a conservative America is a fascist America. He provides no evidence, only cultural cues: people waving flags patriotically, being pro-life, supporting law enforcement, or believing their nation has moral significance. Doing this, he implies traditional values and national pride form, by default, a dangerous concoction.

But this is precisely backward.

Classical conservatism—with its emphasis on limited government, constitutionalism, the rule of law, religious liberty, and decentralization—has always been the antidote to fascism. It stands in direct opposition to the unchecked collectivist dogma and suppression of dissent that defined true fascist regimes. But this remains hidden to the students because Britt, and therefore the teacher, never actually defines fascism. Real fascism is not even close to cultural or political conservatism. It is, as historian Stanley Payne described, "a political system marked by authoritarian centralism, suppression of pluralism, militant nationalism directed by the state, and the eradication of dissent."[7] Fascism's ultimate goal is to silence dissent and to achieve ideological conformity.

Admittedly, an honest view of contemporary America does show these tactics being employed—but not by conservatives. It was the Biden administration that had to issue formal apologies and fund settlements for weaponizing the IRS. Indeed, the IRS admitted to targeting conservative groups for additional scrutiny based on their political beliefs. The case of *Linchpins of Liberty v. United States* is just one example.[8] After Elon Musk purchased Twitter, countless documents were released (the "Twitter Files") showing the company coordinated and complied with federal requests to suppress conservative accounts.[9] Those accounts were subjected to "visibility filtering" to limit their reach on the platform.

The same federal agencies pressed other platforms like YouTube and PayPal to de-platform and demonetize conservative accounts under vaguely written policy violations.[10] Closer to home, Biden's Department of Justice labeled protesting parents at school board meetings as "domestic terrorists."[11] Some were arrested, simply for speaking out against allowing boys into girls' locker rooms.[12]

These are not fascist traits emerging from among conservatives. They are tactics being wielded against them.

In short, Britt's article is little more than ideological doctrines masquerading as concerned analysis. It is a sermon designed to influence. By sharing its fourteen signs as definitive, the teacher betrays an intention to use her influence to recraft youthful minds accordingly.

This is not teaching. It is propaganda.

In the end, I met with the school administration. They were polite. They listened. A week-long review ensued. Ultimately, the administration defended the teacher's use of the article. I was offered the chance to move my daughter to another class. I declined, knowing the social consequences would land squarely on her shoulders. Ultimately, the teacher chose to leave the class and was replaced by a permanent substitute.

Trust I am not finished with this situation. Nor is this book.

I begin with this story because it encapsulates the purpose of the following works. What happened to my daughter is a snapshot of a much broader struggle.

The classroom. The courthouse. The newsroom. The workplace. The grocery store. The movie theater. The Church.

These and so many more are fields of battle in the same spiritual and cultural conflict. If we do not know or are not willing to recognize how the Gospel intersects with these arenas—if such ignorance imputes to us a refusal to engage—we will find our children, our freedoms, and our faith reshaped by those who are only too eager to define "truth" on our behalf.

The answer to this is by no means rage. But it isn't a retreat, either. It is clarity concerning Christian identity, the substance that establishes the distinctiveness, and the courage to carry it into the field.

This book is a call to faithful Christian existence in the public square—not based on passing political strategy or wobbly platitudes but grounded in the enduring truth of the Gospel. What follows will seek to confront the myths, expose the threats, and build up the people of God for engagement—daringly faithful, confessional, and entirely Christ-centered.

It's likely you'll notice along the way my preferred style of communication is storytelling. Jesus told stories. Those stories—the parables—played no small role in the ruling authorities wanting Him dead. For example, they knew what He meant when He described a landowner sending servants and eventually his son to collect fruit from tenant farmers, how they abused and killed the ones sent (Luke 20:9–19). They knew what Jesus meant because they knew the facts of Israel's history and recognized the doctrinal premises inherent to the Lord's message.

Stories have a way of steering straight through our defenses undetected and then, suddenly, we're captured by truth. I intend to proceed in this way.

Accordingly, the first two sections of chapters will wrestle with the headier material. As I said before, there is substance establishing Christian distinctiveness, and it desperately needs parsing. There are historical and theological premises that must be iterated before the stories can rightly capture. Nevertheless, each of those chapters will conclude with a pastoral reflection. These reflections are not tangents but intentional ponderings—moments drawn from ministry and life embodying the truths explored in the material preceding it. They serve as a means of incarnation, bringing the theological and historical to bear in the tangible world of classrooms, courtrooms, sanctuaries, and supper tables.

You'll notice the final four chapters depart from this pattern. They contain no separate pastoral reflections. That's not because the storytelling has ended but because those chapters are the reflections. By the time you arrive there, the groundwork will have been laid. The arguments will have been made. What remains is the deeper call: to live the truth, to walk it in courage, to suffer for it, and, should God require it, to die in the hope it brings.

God willing, all three sections will form a coherent whole—one that understands the world my daughter is growing up in will not pause for cowardice. And besides, the Gospel does not allow it, anyway.

Section 1

Chapter 1

Eroded Foundations

The Church stands at a pivotal crossroads. Once a principal shaper of the nation's moral and civic landscape, its influence is receding. This retreat is not merely cultural or political; it is theological. At stake is the very identity and mission of the Church as a truth-bearing body in the public square. Before this reality can be rightly addressed, it must first be acknowledged. What follows is a sobering observance—not necessarily through the eyes of its critics but through the lens of its own self-disclosure and doctrinal confession. Here begins a necessary confrontation with the uncomfortable truths threatening to render the Church irrelevant, not by force from without but by erosion from within.

Evidence of this ecclesial retreat is already visible in America's Church bodies. My own denomination, the Lutheran Church–Missouri Synod (LCMS), is no exception.[1] Conversely, the secular sphere continues to expand and occupy the Church's former fields of influence. Levels of dogmatic abidance indicate the shift. For example, the LCMS is by its official doctrine an unreservedly pro-life denomination. As a result, one might estimate only a splinter of its members to be pro-choice. And yet, this is not the case. In a recent Pew Research poll, while 51 percent of LCMS members were accounted as pro-life, 46 percent held pro-choice ideologies.[2] These statistics are telling, and as researcher and sociologist Steve Bruce has long since established, are relative to secularism's encroachment—namely, the gradual society-level blending of life's various endeavors eventually neutering religion's lens-like usefulness.[3]

As Christianity's basic theologies erode, becoming for its members more so extra-curricular than essential, other topics are equally threatened and gradually redefined. Religious liberty is one such topic. In part, the innards of this thesis will reveal these trajectories. Furthermore, it will surmise the American Church's clergy and church members (parishioners) as blameworthy.

Concerning parishioners, the converse movements are often imperceptible—a relatively undetectable slow-boil confusing their role as Christians in the public square. For the Church, the public square is a crucial temporal arena for maintaining religious liberty protections. However, because parishioners often lack doctrinal content while being uninformed and desensitized to the dangers, the primary responsibility for combatting the erosion rests with the clergy (Acts 20:28; Eph. 4:11–13). The problem is many Christians do not engage in the public square because pastors fail to demonstrate and clearly communicate the engagement's importance.

This is not a new concern. While away in France during the Constitutional Convention of 1787, Thomas Jefferson sent a letter of concern to James Madison. In the correspondence, Jefferson wrote that the document being birthed did not have "a bill of rights providing clearly, without the aid of sophism, for freedom of religion."[4] Madison should have expected nothing less from his friend. Jefferson long considered religious liberty "the most inalienable and sacred of all human rights."[5]

Going forward, this volume operates on the basis of several foundational expectations. The first bears Jefferson's geist, which is religious liberty is sacred and salutary and, therefore, worth preserving. This is true because its security benefits all citizens despite their religious affiliation or spiritual devotion. In tandem, this notion understands the opposing ideology, which warns of potential Church and State cross-contamination.

In a guest essay for *The New York Times*, Lindsay F. Wiley writes similarly, arguing how religious liberty provisions pose nothing short of an existential threat to public wellbeing, especially as certain faith groups refuse vaccinations considered essential to community health.[6] Unfortunately, these perspectives, and others like them, remain largely undercooked, missing religious liberty's primary thrust.

To accept religious liberty as a societal-wide benefit and then to pursue its preservation is to acknowledge its two-way labors to protect religious and non-religious alike. In other words, this effort assumes religious liberty protects the citizen's conscience, sheltering it from religious imposition. In a practical sense, and by example, this means a Christian juggler cannot be compelled to perform at a homosexual wedding just as a homosexual juggler cannot be compelled to perform at a Christian carnival celebrating biblical marriage. Religious liberty provides equal footing to both ideologies, preventing either belief system from claiming an intrinsic dominance requiring those beyond its borders to conform.

Yet even with such legal and philosophical clarity, the defense of religious liberty must remain more than an abstract or theoretical endeavor. It must be shepherded in real time by real pastors among real people—people whose understanding of Christian doctrine, cultural engagement, and ecclesial authority is often more fragile than assumed. The following offers a lived example of just how these challenges surface within the life of the Church, revealing not only the cultural confusion pervading the pews but the costly assumptions too easily made from the pulpit.

Pastoral Reflection: Three Assumptions Too Many

Several years ago, a member of my congregation—never particularly regular in attendance, though familiar enough—left a voicemail signaling something was amiss. When I returned her call, it quickly became clear her concern wasn't tied to any singular event but was instead the result of a long-simmering grievance. She wanted me to know, in no uncertain terms, she considered me a "rotten pastor" and had little appreciation for the Church since the departure of my predecessor.

As the conversation unfolded, however, a deeper issue began to emerge—one having less to do with personal dislike and more to do with discomfort over what she perceived to be the politicization of the pulpit. She expressed her growing weariness with what she called "politicized topics" in sermons and letters, especially those touching on abortion, homosexuality, and transgenderism. These were, in her estimation, issues the Bible did not address in the way the Church claimed.

Despite the fact that I had never once preached topically—always adhering to the lectionary texts and engaging them exegetically—she remained convinced I was imposing a political agenda. The final straw, she said was a congregational letter including comments from our Synodical President regarding religious liberty. As far as she was concerned, this confirmed her suspicions. She asked to be released from membership.

The exchange was more than a disagreement—it was revelatory. It exposed at least three dangerous assumptions I had been making in my work as a preacher and teacher, the first of which was especially convicting.

The Pastor Is God's Messenger of Truth

I labored under the assumption the people I served actually regarded me as one called by God to speak truth—objectively, authoritatively, and with an expectation of holistic alignment. I presumed when I preached, the hearer would at least wrestle with the question: "What is God saying to me through His servant by way of His holy Word?" But what I failed to account for was a more likely question in today's ecclesial climate: "How can I assimilate what God is supposedly saying through this pastor into what I already believe to be true, so I can continue to do what I do and believe what I believe?"

In twenty-first-century American Christendom, the latter question, it seems, is far more common than the former.

Alignment with the Church's Doctrinal Beliefs

The second presumption: Regular church attendance within a conservative denomination like the LCMS indicated a baseline of biblical orthodoxy. In other words, I assumed those active in LCMS congregations were, by default, in relative alignment with the Church's public confession. After all, the doctrinal distance between the LCMS and a more theologically liberal body such as the Evangelical Lutheran Church in America (ELCA) is not insignificant. But that distinction, while clear on paper, can be far less pronounced in practice.[7]

Multiple cultural factors—perhaps most notably, radical individualism—are increasingly blurring these lines. As a result, the biblical "givens" shaping LCMS positions on topics like abortion, homosexuality, and gender identity are often either unknown to the average member or have already been filtered through a secular ethos. Within that ethos, such topics are no longer seen as theological matters but as private, moral opinions. Consequently, the assumption that someone's affiliation with a particular synod is a reliable indicator of their doctrinal alignment is no longer a safe bet.

Group and Personal Bible Study

The third presumption was equally consequential: Recipients of the preached Word were not only exposed to ample opportunities for corporate study but also engaged in regular personal reading of the Scriptures. I presumed a degree of biblical familiarity such that controversial topics, when encountered in the pulpit, would be navigable—perhaps even welcomed—as clarifying applications of God's Word. But research continues to show a steep decline in both communal and individual Bible study across American congregations. The net result is a generation of hearers unfamiliar with the Scriptures, understanding God and His will primarily through the lens of culture rather than the Bible's own self-description.[8]

The erosion of theological clarity and conviction among self-identified Christians is not a peripheral concern. It is the root system from which broader societal shifts draw their momentum. If the Church cannot discern or defend what is true, then it will not long endure as the steward of truth. The data presented here, while disheartening, do not signal inevitability. They signal urgency. The Church must reckon with its internal compromise before it can speak with credibility to the world. In the following chapters, we will examine how this compromise took root—not only theologically but sociologically and institutionally—uncovering the contours of what many now call the Church's "Great Decline," and how attempts to arrest this downward course have often misdiagnosed the source. Only by rightly diagnosing the decline can we begin to recover the clarity, courage, and confession necessary for exacting the Church's crucial role in the public square.

❧

Chapter 2

The False Memory of a Godless Republic

Having exposed the internal compromises weakening the Church's public witness, we now turn to the broader cultural and institutional realities reflecting and accelerating this retreat. Sociologists, theologians, and public intellectuals have labored to understand the Church's place in a rapidly shifting world—a task made more urgent by the collapse of its former influence.

Plentiful sweat has been shed studying what many researchers would call Christianity's "Great Decline."[1] Craig A. Carter,[2] David Fowler, along with Jon and Jill Musgrave,[3] and Michael Levitt[4] are a few notable commenters.[5] The fact Christianity is receding into the public square's shadows in America is by no means new information. Although, the resultant pace and its products remain in flux; suggesting to the hopeful a turnaround is entirely possible.[6] But many of the Church's proposed turnarounds, often packaged in new programs and church growth models, reveal a narrow focus—one mistaking external expansion for internal health.

To that end, Christianity's various branches continue to extend themselves into this program and that model, all led by "experts" intending to halt the decline and return to health, which, for many, is often only concerned with local congregational growth rather than engagement with culture.[7] Within these grand measures, communication is often heralded as key. Indeed, there is the insistence that the Church's identity and mission must be articulated before its members can go forth equipped with the eternal message that saves.[8]

The Church's struggle with cultural relevance cannot be solved by rebranding or programming alone. Its health will depend on a renewed grasp of identity—one expressed not just in institutional form but through its faithful proclamation and presence in the world. In the next chapter, we will consider how this reclamation begins with the vocational self-understanding of clergy as both theological stewards and civic shepherds.

In his volume *The Picture of Dorian Gray*, Oscar Wilde makes an intuitive remark through the character of Lord Henry Wotton. Responding to Gray's insistence he stay while Basil Hallward paints his portrait, Wotton replies, "to influence a person is to give him one's own soul."[9] His words not only tease the forthcoming narrative but with incredible brevity, they establish influence's potency and reach. Indeed, influence involves transferring one's innermost to another in ways that shape his or her being. The following sections will consider principal perspectives concerning early America's fundamental influences.

That historical conversation is not merely academic. Its consequences echo today in places like Oregon, where Christian families are now told they cannot adopt children unless they affirm gender ideologies directly contradicting their faith. Such modern developments reveal just how far the narrative has shifted—and why the question of our founding influences still matters deeply.

To be perplexed by Christianity's declining influence in America is to accept the possibility it existed muscularly before. Erwin Chemerinsky, a progressive constitutionalist, argues against the premise's verity entirely, noting not only that America is not a Christian nation and "should never be considered one" but that the Enlightenment, bolstered by human reason and combined with the desire to avoid theocratic governance, was and continues to be America's chief influence.[10]

Montverde Academy's Tiffany E. Piland surmises similarly in her master's thesis: "Overall, the American founders were molded by the period of Enlightenment. Influenced by the lives of Enlightenment writers and their works, the founders were encouraged to question authority figures and traditional institutions. This led to the invocation of reason and rationality, both of which had a profound impact on the formation of an independent America."[11]

Distinguished professor of British history at the University of Kansas, J. C. D. Clark, appears to agree, insisting the Enlightenment's powerful grip influenced the theological positions that make the American and French Revolutions possible. Surveying the influence of Richard Price—a Welsh Nonconformist minister and someone well-connected to the likes of Benjamin Franklin, George Washington, John Adams, and Benjamin Rush[12]—Clark shows Price's repeated insistence the Church was emerging from an age of darkness trapped in tradition. For Price, the emergence would result in a distinct separation between Church and State. Although, Price never fully described or understood the separation's eventual parameters.[13]

This effort does not argue the Founders sought to establish a theocracy, nor that Christianity reigned without challenge. Rather, it challenges the increasingly popular myth the American founding was purely secular or uniformly deist. That myth, now used to marginalize the Church's presence in public life, rests on revisionist readings of history that obscure the genuine theological commitments of many early leaders.

Provost of Concordia University in Mequon, Wisconsin, William R. Cario, would say little has changed. As with Clark's more recent determination and Price's historical one, Cario defined the Enlightenment's relationship with the Church in two ways back in 1999. First, Cario noted its inherent distrust of tradition, citing such examples as Isaac Newton, who insisted things be empirically tested rather than simply trusting the Church's longstanding explanations. Second, Cario pointed to Thomas Hobbes and John Locke. As early American influencers (likely familiar with Richard Price's writings), Hobbes and Locke sought to disregard the common religious mandates for government and instead locate its authority in a citizenry comprised of individuals bearing free will.[14]

Like Clark and Cario, emeritus professor of religious studies at the College of William and Mary, David L. Holmes likewise believes the nation's founders were enlightened men of reason and distrustful of Christianity, actively laboring against its influence in public affairs.[15] In his volume *Pagans and Christians in the City: Culture Wars from the Tiber to the Potomac*, Steven D. Smith presents a derivative of Holmes's, Clark's, and Cario's cases. Smith admits Christianity had a strong influence. However, the Founders deliberately avoided any significant recognition of it, choosing instead an agnostic path, avoiding the Christian and secular labels.[16]

Geoffrey Stone, a University of Chicago law professor, insists deism is America's essential framework.[17] Christopher Grasso, author of *Skepticism and American Faith: From the Revolution to the Civil War*, believes this only in part, choosing to steer back toward the Enlightenment. Admitting deism was influential, Grasso claims Christianity's influence outweighed it by far, nearly labeling it anathema. Grasso does tip his hat to deism for cementing free speech and debate as central to American life. Nevertheless, Grasso builds as Clark does, asserting early American Christianity was overtly shaped by the Enlightenment, pointing to instances betraying contention between established religious practices and individual liberties.[18]

These assessments reveal a complex interplay between Enlightenment rationalism, deistic influence, and Christian tradition. But were these ideological streams equally formative—or does the record suggest a more dominant religious current beneath the surface?

Much closer to the Great Decline's beginning in the 1960s, Paul F. Boller's seminal volume *George Washington & Religion* (which presented a relatively radical perspective by comparison to what came before) contended alongside Stone, writing how America's first president was more influenced by the principles of deism (and its connection to reason) than his Christian affiliations.[19]

Perhaps circumstantially, researcher Shun-hing Chan notes it was during the civil rights movement in America in the 1960s when initial attempts at critical research concerning clergy and politics were stirred. The relatively new perspective's goal was to understand the relationship between theology and the clergy's personal political convictions. Chan notes this research has continued in America, only within the past twenty years becoming more concerned with religion's over-arching civic influence, implying that before the 1960s, the Church's influence in the public square was assumed, expected, and largely unchallenged.[20]

By contrast, plenty of respected observers differ from those previously mentioned. For example, Gary DeMar makes a case for America's distinctly Christian roots, noting the faith communities of the first colonies held the greatest sway for unifying the new nation.[21] Writer and historian William J. Federer spends 845 pages on direct quotations from early American sources highlighting Christianity's direct impact on the nation. Within, he recommends reading from notable figures such as Jedediah Morse, the author of *Annals of the American Revolution* (originally published in 1824), who wrote a few short years after the Revolutionary War, "To the kindly influence of Christianity we owe the degree of civil freedom, and political and social happiness which mankind now enjoys."[22]

Tracing Federer's plentiful citations to their sources, one can engage with original documents and discover broader examinations by those who were present when America was founded. For example, after a visit to and an extensive study of America, Alexis de Tocqueville, the French historian and philosopher, produced the monumental work *Democracy in America.* Within, he concluded America's highest authority was unarguably the Christian religion, noting it as the truest reason for the new nation's enlightenment.[23]

Perhaps just as convincing, John Quincy Adams, the sixth president of the United States, recalled poetically how America's birth "is indissolubly linked with the birthday of the Savior. The Declaration of Independence laid the cornerstone of human government upon the first precepts of Christianity."[24]

The Heritage Foundation's Mark David Hall resides between the two perspectives, offering critically that those who wholly deny the possibility of Christianity's influence and those who embrace it without pause skew the Founders' intentions. Hall insists neither of these absolutist positions accommodates historical context, which, from his perspective, includes precise doctrinal positions capable of disqualifying membership in certain branches of Christianity, thereby negating their technical influence. In other words, a Calvinist might claim one who denies the doctrine of double predestination is not a Christian, just as a Lutheran might claim one who denies Christ's vicarious atonement is outside the faith. Only a splinter of America might be considered Christian by those oft-iterated denominational metrics.

Reasonably, then, Hall prefers to conclude Christian ideologies likely influenced the Founders in a subjective sense, that is, in the same way nominal and orthodox Christians might be considered influenced by their religion's doctrines.[25] Hall's conclusion assists, if only to clarify. The concern is not for proving national Christian conception but for measures of legitimate influence. On the other hand, author and historian Eric Metaxas insists everything that made America, including its essential role in the world, "had everything to do with our churches, or with the American church."[26] By this, Metaxas claims the Church has a rightful place at the civic table.

Pastoral Reflection: From Rev. Jason Lee to Oregon Today

Today, in states like Oregon, Christians are being told they may not adopt children unless they affirm the state's radical gender ideology.[27] This isn't a marginal issue; it is a sharp and present example of the Church being told to sit down and be quiet.

Ironically, Oregon would not be what it is without the influence of Christian conviction. Rev. Jason Lee, a Methodist missionary, once stood at the center of efforts to bring Oregon into the Union, believing that aligning with the United States would aid the spread of the Gospel among Native Americans.[28] The American government followed his lead. A Christian pastor helped shape a state's destiny because he believed the Gospel belonged not just in the pulpit but in the public square.

This kind of influence—Christians engaging boldly in the nation's formation—raises serious questions about the now-popular claim that religion, particularly Christianity, was never meant to shape public life in America. The further I explored this theme, the more frequently I encountered one particular assertion, repeated with academic certainty but built on sand.

While not necessarily central to this book's effort, one relatively widespread speculation that must be handled accordingly is the assertion that America's founding fathers were principally deists. This matters because the credibility of the separationist claim—the Church must remain detached from public life—often hinges on the belief the Founders held to a detached, deistic worldview. If that belief is unfounded or exaggerated, the modern arguments for strict separation are built on a distorted understanding of the nation's origins.

Interestingly, the full-throttle deist proposition doesn't appear on the scene until the early to mid-twentieth century and only then does it become a tactic more than a truth. In other words, the folks pressing for absolute separationism (the complete removal of the Church's voice in the public square) were the ones driving the idea.

Admittedly, it is true some of the Founders were deists. Still, that needs clarification. The term "deism" wasn't really in use during the time of the American Revolution. While there were indeed individuals who held deistic beliefs—some of whom were quite notable—even when the term was used, it didn't have the same connotations or associations as it does today. That's important.

Today, deism is plainly associated with a specific set of beliefs. For example, deists believe while God created the universe, He doesn't intervene in human affairs. Deists also deny the divinity of Christ, along with countless other cultic dogmas. However, even the prominent Founders, so often labeled devout deists, didn't actually believe these things during the American Revolution. Some did. But most didn't.

In certain respects, that disqualifies the label's application. But to learn these things, more than internet snippets are required. You need time with what they and their observing biographers recorded. As with Rev. Jason Lee, there are plentiful opinions concerning his reasons for engaging in governmental affairs. And yet, his diary remains a far better source than an onlooking professor from the 1960s.

Even beyond the usual suspects, most Founders responsible for the nation's design—many of whom are unknown by comparison to the usual suspects—did the heavy lifting.[29] They were crucial in designing and building the American ship, hoisting its sails, and putting it to sea. The majority was unequivocally Christian.[30] Not Muslim. Not Jewish. Not Buddhist. Christian.

That's not being exclusionist. It's simply being honest. From the authors of the founding documents to the signers, ratifying delegates, justices, cabinet secretaries, and military leaders, these individuals were a diverse mix of creedal believers and clergy from various Christian denominations. Did they have doctrinal differences among them? Yes. Still, they confessed the triune God, proclaimed Christ as the divine Son of God and the essentiality of faith in Him for salvation, held fast to the sacramental things as the mysteriously miraculous gifts they are, and so on.

To ignore this broad and sincere Christian consensus is not merely an oversight—it's a distortion with consequences. If these truths are obscured or erased, it becomes far easier to advance the notion the Founders intended a purely secular public square.

Furthermore, an honest historian won't centralize and therefore label a nation's innermost identity and destiny based on the ideologies of its minority. But a dishonest one would. Indeed, a dishonest one would insist America was founded on deism and use similar revisions to sever the Church from the nation's public life. It's not just an error of historical interpretation—it's a deliberate strategy to strip away any legitimate claim Christians might have to speak into the nation's moral and civic conscience.

And there you have it—a postmodern, radically individualized America separated from her genuine identity and more easily susceptible to false narratives. A man can be a woman. All white people are inherently racist. Murdering unborn babies is healthcare. The Church has no right to influence political discussion. And so on.

It doesn't have to be this way. The destabilizing minority was no match for the majority, even if only a portion of the majority had the slightest fraction of the Founders' courage to speak and act. However, silence has become the norm, and courage is now viewed as extremism. The result is a vacuum—one the enemies of truth are more than willing to fill.

But that'll forever be a problem—especially when the seeds of America's garden, the churches, are tended by pastors who have embraced the lie. Instead of standing guard over truth, too many now echo the very separationist claims designed to silence them. And when the shepherds retreat, the wolves do not hesitate.

I recently told my youngest daughter, Evelyn, the story of Major General (John) Peter Muhlenberg. When she heard how Muhlenberg, a Lutheran pastor, stood before his congregation and preached in a way that inspired the men of his congregation to join him in the fight, she felt a strange craving to read all about him.[31] I've since given her a few books. She's going to discover along the way one unique detail. She's going to learn about Peter's brother, Frederick, a pastor in New York. Frederick was not happy with Peter. He believed the Church, especially her ministers, had no right to speak about, let alone engage in, civil affairs. He openly denounced his brother's enthusiasm on multiple occasions.

But then, one day, the British surrounded Frederick's church and burned it to the ground. The moment forced a reckoning. Rev. Frederick Muhlenberg, once a vocal opponent of his brother's civic engagement, reversed course.[32] He went on to become the first Speaker of the United States House of Representatives, ultimately championing the cause he once condemned—the necessity of the Church's voice in the life of the nation.[33] He learned the importance of public engagement the hard way—by watching his sanctuary burn. Tragically, pastors and churches in twenty-first-century America appear poised to learn the same lesson, just as painfully.

Remember Oregon. Christian parents there must now sign a state-imposed agreement affirming radical gender ideology before they can adopt. But no faithful Christian can do that in good conscience. So what are they to do? Leave the state? Break the law? Abandon the hope of adoption entirely? In every scenario, they are already being forced into the margins—already living in the shadows. And perhaps it didn't have to come to this. Perhaps a bolder, clearer Christian voice—one like Rev. Jason Lee's—could have kept the floodgates shut. But when

Christians, and especially their pastors, buy into the radical left's insistence that the Church must remain silent in civil affairs, it is not neutrality that results—it is collapse. And the collapse always favors those most eager to erase the truth.

The narrative that America was never shaped by Christianity is not only historically flimsy—it's strategically destructive. If Christians accept it, they will cede the public square to those most committed to their silence. But the truth reveals something different: that faithful engagement was present at the founding, and it must be present now. If the Church is to reclaim its voice, it must begin with those called to lead it. And that begins with the clergy.

☙

Chapter 3

Rooted in Another Kingdom

If the Church is to reclaim its public voice, it must begin with its leaders. This requires rethinking the pastoral office, not only as a theological vocation but as a civic one. To that end, both domestic and international studies reveal what is often overlooked in Western discourse.

Applying the prospects of American research to churches in Hong Kong, Shun-hing Chan acknowledges, "researchers need to understand both the religious contexts and the broader non-ecclesiastical contexts that shape clergy's political participation."[1] This is to ask: When clergy appear to engage or disengage, is either dimension fully understood? Are they being theological, political, or cross-platforming in ways considered faithful to their understanding of Church and State?

Whatever the interpretive framework, one thing remains clear: The office of pastor has historically included public consequence. Executive Director of the Washington Theological Consortium, Larry A. Golemon, asserts history's proofs, noting the early "theological schools knew how important the office of clergy was—as a religious and public profession."[2] Golemon compares the early schools to the modern ones emerging in the late twentieth century, showing how the later models are strictly concerned with theology and its technique, while the earlier schools were broader in scope, often training their students as public servants geared toward serving in their communities.

Earlier schools delivered crisp familiarity with and engagement in various fields such as medicine, law, and educational pedagogy. In other words, the clergy were indeed cross-platforming, understanding themselves to be just as much a part of society's structural landscape as lawyers, doctors, and teachers, together considered essential threads within the societal fabric.

Concerning clergy influence, Golemon adds that it happened by way of inspirational rhetoric and oration. Here, Golemon acknowledges the clergy's monumental impact rooted in the use of language and its social transmissibility. He later clarifies how the influence was primarily flexed through public media outlets such as journals and magazines, also noting abundant participation in public addresses, organizations with national scope, and other activities directly influencing public life.[3]

Eric Metaxas posits likewise, referencing the all but practical importance of clergy involvement throughout history, calling attention to the need for the Church's voice in contexts ruled by the likes of Adolph Hitler and Mao Zedong.[4] He goes further, naming prominent pastors who engaged directly with the public square for change, that is, countless pastors who spoke against King George III's colonial abuses in the eighteenth century, as well as Dietrich Bonhoeffer's stance against Nazism in 1930s Germany, and William Wilberforce's nineteenth-century work to abolish the slave trade.[5]

And yet for all these powerful precedents, the Church today often defaults to shallower ground when public confrontation comes.

Pastoral Reflection: Anchored Beyond the Amendment

One modern episode illustrates the fragility of the Church's public witness when it is grounded more in civil liberties than in eternal truths.

A particularly revealing moment of modern clergy response occurred in October 2014, when a pastor in Houston, Texas, declared, "I'm going to stand firm in the faith. It is my First Amendment right!" The catalyst was a controversial non-discrimination ordinance passed by the Houston City Council allowing individuals identifying as transgender to use public bathrooms aligned with their gender identity.[6] Many citizens objected and organized a petition to overturn the ordinance. Strangely, the petition was ultimately annulled, even though it received nearly 50,000 signatures, which was more than twice the required 17,269.[7]

The controversy deepened when the openly gay mayor, Annise Parker, sought and secured subpoenas for sermons and private correspondence from certain Houston pastors, seeking to verify they had not engaged in discriminatory speech.[8] To many observers, this felt like a scene lifted directly from Orwell's *1984*, a dystopia in which government-controlled ministries manipulated truth and punished dissenting expression. What stirred the most concern for me, however, was not simply the city council's actions—though deeply troubling—but the nature of the public defense.

In the wake of national attention and the opportunity to testify to something greater, I found the responses to be narrowly framed. I read very little other than the First Amendment as the grounds for resistance. In my opinion, this was a missed opportunity.

While fighting for one's right to free speech is constitutionally sound, it raises a deeper question: What happens when such legal protections no longer exist? What if, like Christians under Nero or citizens under totalitarian regimes, legal recourse is altogether nonexistent?

Before going any further in the work, we must agree that true strength in the cause for religious liberty doesn't emerge from constitutional permissions but from steadfast Christian conviction. The First Amendment is a blessing, yes. But our call to stand firm in the faith is not born from within it. Rather, it is born from an otherworldly substance—eternal truth—giving rise to protections like the First Amendment in the first place. It is divine revelation, not human legislation, that animates our courage and defines our resolve.

Such a truth shapes how Christians have historically understood their relationship to earthly powers. This is why the apostle Paul's exhortation in Romans 13:1, "Let every person be subject to the governing authorities," often carries strange weight. He wrote those words under Nero, a ruler infamous for his cruelty toward Christians. And yet, even as Paul urged submission to temporal power, he also proclaimed the greater power at work: "I am not ashamed of the gospel, for it is the power of God for salvation . . ." (Rom. 1:16). He reminded the believers in Rome their true security was not found in the decrees of emperors but in the unshakable love of Christ, from which nothing—not death, demons, nor any created thing—could separate them (Rom. 8:38–39).

Paul fortified his readers for engaging in civic life with the Gospel, which transcends the authority of any empire.

That same Gospel compels Christians today with no less resolve. If imprisonment comes, if martyrdom looms, let it be for fidelity to Christ—not for the defense of rights but for faithfulness to the crucified and risen Lord. Let it be because we refuse to forsake our Savior, because the Church cannot be overcome, and because death holds no dominion over her children.

Of course, this does not mean disengagement from public life. The doctrine of the Two Kingdoms (which will be discussed later in this volume) insists Christians live as citizens of both the temporal and spiritual realms. Indeed, legal means should be used to preserve and protect, as Paul did in Acts 25 when he appealed to Caesar. Preserving our rights is wise and just. But let's be clear: The Church's endurance has never depended on earthly rights. It endures because Christ promised it: "The gates of hell shall not prevail against it" (Matt. 16:18), and "Death is swallowed up in victory" (1 Cor. 15:54).

This unshakable confidence does not remove us from civic concern; rather, it roots us more deeply in it. Still, when this confidence wanes—when the Church forgets her otherworldly foundation—an icy stillness begins to descend. The next chapter will explore how cultural ideologies challenge the Church's presence and how pastors must resist accommodation without forfeiting love.

Chapter 4

From Influence to Irrelevance

The diminishing vision for the pastoral office as both a theological and civic calling has broader implications. As clergy retreat from public engagement, the Church becomes less visible in the communal and cultural square. This vocational reductionism has contributed to a larger trend: the Church's declining influence on the very societies it once helped shape. To understand the full breadth of this trend, one must turn to its cultural indicators and societal perceptions, both historical and current.

Various thinkers have attempted to diagnose Christianity's decline. While perspectives differ, all acknowledge the Church's cultural position has drastically changed—moving from the center to the margins.

Professor of Faith and Culture at St. Patrick's College in Maynooth, Ireland, Michael A. Conway, concedes the interweaving of Christianity as influential in the social fabric, writing, "I cannot speak about the church as a reality in our culture in any real way if I do so as a place apart, a special group, or a privileged instance in history."[1] Paradoxically, he affirms this historically even as he admits to the Great Decline, concluding Christianity no longer holds the stabilizing position it once did.[2] Dean of the School of Divinity at African Christian University, the late Voddie T. Baucham Jr., appeared to agree Christianity is waning, and yet, its historical footprint forever proves its value, having "produced the highest levels of freedom and prosperity and the lowest levels of corruption and oppression in the world . . ."[3]

Editor for *The Washington Examiner* and a visiting fellow at the American Enterprise Institute, Timothy P. Carney believes as Conway and Baucham, noting the Church, even as she wanes, is no insignificant force in society.[4] Considering Robert Putnam's work, *American Grace: How Religion Divides and Unites Us*,[5] Carney discovers further agreement. Carney summarizes Putnam's premise, saying he reaffirms the Church as a civil society's most vital institution because its stabilizing effects reach beyond its own membership.[6]

A respected authority on Christian worldview, in his volume, *Truth Changes Everything: How People of Faith Can Transform the World in Times of Crisis*, Jeff Myers helps to further establish Putnam's premise, digging deeper into the soil of world history to name several Christian figures who influenced the world's view of human value in ways still resonating today. Thomas Aquinas, Catherine of Sienna, and Boethius are a few.[7]

While the societal influence of the Church remains significant, the question becomes more focused: What role must pastors play in reversing the decline?

Considering the typical pastor's skill set—such as hermeneutics, homiletics, pedagogy and andragogy, counseling, administration, and the like, all of which are tools accumulated at the seminary for service to the Gospel and the subsequent demonstration of that Gospel in and through real people (Matt. 5:13–16)—it becomes perplexing, then, how waning Christian influence (or engagement) in the public square could hardly be plausible.[8] And yet, it is. The Pew Research Center reported in September of 2022, while 63 percent of U.S. adults identify as Christian (representing a slight change from 2021 but a significant decrease since the decline became noticeable in the 1960s),[9] just one year earlier, more than 55 percent of all U.S. adults expressed strong support for the separation of Church and State,[10] with "separation" implying a much stricter majority opposing religious voices in the public square.[11]

Michael Conway observes the change, writing, "Over the last thirty years or so there has been an enormous shift in our culture, where religion has gone from being centre stage to being a marginal or at least a limited player in terms of society at large."[12] He goes on to say, "Church leadership can no longer dictate political, educational, or social policy, as would have been the case, say, fifty years ago."[13]

Put simply, with the decline in Christianity's population and influence, there is a natural inverse of opposition to Christianity's voice in local, state, and national affairs. Pew Research's numbers suggest this is due, in part, to Christians. In tandem, the Cultural Research Center's *American Worldview Inventory 2022* posited a dreadfully low biblical worldview among key demographics served by Christian churches. The inventory shows: "men (2%), women (4%), whites (4%), blacks (2%), Hispanics (less than one-half of one percent), and less than one-half of 1 percent among those who identify as LGBTQ."[14]

Coincidentally, the American Culture & Faith Institute performed a study in 2015 effectively showing that while 90 percent of conservative pastors believe the Bible speaks to cultural issues such as same-sex marriage, abortion, religious freedom, and the like, approximately 6 percent of the agreeable pastors confessed to preaching sermons or teaching lessons on the topics.[15] In the same survey, 65 percent of congregation respondents wanted "more information from their church about what the Bible teaches in relation to current social and political issues."[16]

In short, the report reveals a crucial dissonance: "Pastors agreed that most of the issues tested were critical or very important to America; yet, they had chosen not to address what the Bible teaches about those issues, despite congregations eager to receive such wisdom."[17]

Apart from any notable concerns for dominionistic activism, at a minimum, the points above suggest a discord between belief and action in American Christianity occurring both inside and outside a church's walls. Pastors unwilling to demonstrate and communicate the importance of public square engagement appear to be part of the problem, thereby fostering church members who function in the public square at levels well below America's historical demonstration.

Pastoral Reflection: Prepared to Endure, Resolved to Stand

The previous data alone, though grim, cannot tell the whole story. A deeper truth presses forward: The health of the Church requires spiritual resolve among its members.

Concerning the text of John 15:1–8, Martin Luther once wrote that believers are called to bear fruit so God may be glorified and their obedience seen.[18] In other words, Christ expects His people to step up visibly and faithfully. Faithfulness in the public square can take many forms—most of them quiet, and few of them grandiose. After Netflix launched and defended the show *Cuties*—rightly condemned by many as sexualizing children—countless Christians responded. Though we may not know their names, millions canceled their subscriptions, contributing to a nearly $9 billion drop in market value over just two days.[19] A Texas grand jury even indicted the show.[20]

Yet Christian witness is often much quieter than this. It's seen in mothers and fathers raising their children faithfully, students remaining grounded in hostile classrooms, business owners refusing to compromise their ethics, and church members confronting theological drift. These small acts are not small at all. They are frontline engagements in the broader spiritual conflict—living expressions of Gospel certainty that frustrate the devil precisely because they cannot be shaken.

Luther, in *The Bondage of the Will*, insisted, "The Holy Spirit is no skeptic, and it is not doubts or mere opinions that he has written on our hearts, but assertions more sure and certain than life itself and all experience."[21] He echoed Paul's words in 1 Thessalonians 1:5, where the Gospel comes "not simply with words but also with power . . . and deep conviction" (NIV). The Greek word translated as "conviction," πληροφορίᾳ, means nothing less than full assurance. Paul reiterates this same certainty in Colossians 2:2 and Romans 15:29.

This is why Luther also insisted, "Nothing is better known or more common among Christians than assertion. Take away assertions and you take away Christianity. Why, the Holy Spirit is given them from heaven, that he may glorify Christ in them and confess him even unto death . . ." For Luther, assertion meant far more than intellectual assent. It meant unwavering confidence in God's Word—an unflinching "yes" to Christ and His truth, and a resolute "no" to compromise: Yes, I believe what Christ has said. No, I will not embrace falsehood. Yes, I confess Scripture as the sole source for faith, life, and practice. No, I will not trade it for cultural comfort, even at the cost of career, reputation, or personal peace.

Luther's point is the Holy Spirit does not inspire ambivalence. But is the American Church proving capable of this kind of conviction?

There was an exchange between Dietrich Bonhoeffer and fellow pastor Gerhard Vibrans. Vibrans wrote for advice, lamenting:

> My parish of six hundred souls at Schweinitz . . . on average only one or two people go to church every Sunday. . . . Every Sunday, wearing my vestments, I make a pilgrimage through the whole village primarily

> to bring home to the people that it is Sunday. . . . The people try to comfort me by saying that I will get my salary even though no one goes to church.[22]

Bonhoeffer's response was blunt: "If one village will not listen, we go to another. There are limits."[23]

The blustery winds of disregard for God's Word were already stripping away the summer of His presence, ushering in a deathly winter of His absence.

Bonhoeffer was telling Vibrans what Christ told the first pastors, His disciples, to do in Matthew 10:14. Bonhoeffer's words also walked in stride with Paul's observation in Romans 1:18–32 where the apostle wrote three times of the people who had forsaken God and His Word, saying, "God gave them up . . ." This is particularly important for us to understand, especially since I assume many readers of this book identify as Christian. Paul is warning us in the face of deliberate disregard for God's Word, it is possible after a while that His patience will run out and He'll grant the separation such a rejection proves to desire. Paul warns, God has done it before and He'll do it again. When He does, the summertime of His grace gives way to the awful winter of His absence and everything that comes with it—which is, ultimately, utter destruction of an obstinate people.

Luther wrote something similar to the people of Germany:

> Let us remember our former misery, and the darkness in which we dwelt. Germany, I am sure, has never before heard so much of God's word as it is hearing today; certainly we read nothing of it in history. If we let it just slip by without thanks and honor, I fear we shall suffer a still more dreadful darkness and plague. O my beloved Germans, buy while the market is at your door; gather in the harvest while there is sunshine and fair weather; make use of God's grace and word while it is there! For you should know that God's word

> and grace is like a passing shower of rain which does not return where it has once been.[24]

Luther goes on to share a number of very real examples of this. He notes how the Jews had the pure Word of God once, but now it's absent among them. He noted how Paul carried God's pure Word into the midst of the known Greek world but "now they have the Turk. And you Germans need not think that you will have it forever, for ingratitude and contempt will not make it stay. Therefore, seize it and hold it fast, whoever can; for lazy hands are bound to have a lean year."[25]

Eventually, Bonhoeffer went to visit Vibrans and, after seeing things for himself, he instructed him to write an open letter to the people. In it, he was to make clear it would be the last offer of God's Word to them, reminding them there were plenty of other places hungering for the preaching of the divine truth. Vibrans wrote the letter, and receiving a cold response, he resigned his call and left.[26]

It would be foolish for the American Church to presume God's blessings and freedoms will linger amid spiritual apathy. Too many Christians have grown complacent, mistaking cultural comfort for divine favor. The pandemic did not cause this weakness—it exposed it, revealing a Church too willing to exchange conviction for convenience and passive quietism.

In contrast, believers in the Middle East risk death for the very truths many here are reluctant even to speak. If we persist in cowardice, we should not expect God's continued favor. His patience, though long, is not without end.

To live as a Christian today is to stand visibly and courageously. It means naming abortion as evil, even when it costs us friendships. It means holding to the truth of Scripture when doing so may jeopardize one's career or reputation. This is the shape of faithful endurance in a hostile age. While Christ does say that amid trial we will be given what to say (Matt. 10:18–20), the Scriptures also teach that strength for this endurance does not arise magically apart from substance. It is forged over time through spiritual discipline, tested convictions, and a heart trained to trust the Lord and His Word, regardless of the consequences (1 Tim. 4:7–8; Heb. 12:11; James 1:2–4; Rom. 5:3–4). Indeed, Christ warned in the parable of the Ten Virgins (Matt. 25:1–13), only those with oil—those prepared—will endure.

If the blessings of this land dry up and the winter of judgment descends, it will be the prepared, the faithfully resolved, who endure the storm and live to see the spring of God's deliverance.

But disengagement is only part of the problem. Even among those still in the pews, there is a growing dissonance between professed faith and practiced life. It is not merely how the world has pushed the Church to the margins. It is how many Christians have welcomed the shift by trading biblical clarity for cultural convenience. The next chapter will steer directly into this duplicity.

Chapter 5

FAITH CHOOSES SIDES

While chapter 4 examined the Church's retreat from cultural relevance due to a failure of engagement, what follows is an even deeper concern: the internal compromise of Christians who remain active yet indistinct from the world.

In the wake of the Church's diminishing witness and compromise, voices inside and outside the Church have attempted to diagnose what ails American Christianity. One such voice, Matt Walsh, does so with biting satire. In his book *Church of Cowards: A Wake-Up Call to Complacent Christians*, nationally recognized columnist and podcaster Matt Walsh imagines heathen invaders landing in America, a nation they believed was overwhelmingly Christian, only to discover a startling disconnect between the nation's actual culture and their expectations.

Walsh writes, "They had pictured an America filled with pious, modest, prayerful believers, but instead they find silly, shallow, oversexed, nihilistic zombies . . ."[1] He describes further examples, such as the merciless invaders' shock at doctors removing healthy unborn children in pieces from mothers' wombs.[2] Walsh's point is simple. The distance between what American Christianity believes and does is considerable, and he believes "the church in America is not being killed from outside. The secular, the non-Christian, even the Christian-haters are not destroying us. . . . Rather the church is collapsing because of exactly the kinds of Christians who want Christmas but not Christianity."[3]

In other words, American Christianity has lost its substance and become conformed to the world. Voddie T. Baucham Jr. asserts the same, writing how far too many popular theologians have embraced dangerously suicidal social agendas that disrupt the flow of genuine Christian doctrine, ultimately parting their beliefs from their deeds. For Baucham, Critical Race Theory (CRT) is one such agenda.[4]

This disconnect, while cultural on the surface, is deeply theological. It reveals a Church that has forgotten something fundamental: Faith, by its nature, chooses a side. To follow Christ is to be set against the world's lies. There is no neutrality in the Gospel. As Jesus said, "Whoever is not with me is against me" (Matt. 12:30). And yet, in modern America, many Christians attempt to live between loyalties—hoping to appear faithful without causing offense. But God does not bless half-hearted allegiance. He stands against evil. And so must His people.

Natasha Crain, a former VP of marketing and business development and an adjunct marketing professor at California State University, in her book *Faithfully Different: Regaining Biblical Clarity in a Secular Culture*, assures a church conformed to the world is not anything new. Paul warned against this (Romans 12:2).[5] She logically admits relative to Christianity's current decline that "many of those who are abandoning Christianity are now also abandoning Christian values."[6] But like Walsh, she affirms the need for the remaining Christians' biblical distinctiveness to make sense collectively. She insists for "Christians who seek to have a biblical worldview . . . an a la carte belief system . . . is not an option."[7] In her contribution to *Healing Humanity: Confronting Our Moral Crisis*, Frederica Mathewes-Green describes living up to one's beliefs through demonstrable deeds as the actual test of conviction.[8]

Within the same volume, dean and emeritus professor of moral theology at Holy Trinity Seminary in Jordanville, New York, Alexander F. C. Webster, moves the reticule of conviction toward the public square's encroachment, making plain the need for Christians to act according to faith simply by saying "'No!' to those in positions of power over us who would harass, oppress, or even persecute us for our Orthodox Christian fidelity."[9]

In his article for *Touchstone: A Journal of Mere Christianity*, pastor and commenter Joshua Steely adds to Webster's insistence, writing how the Church may seem defeated by the public square's secular forces, having lost its religious liberty, nevertheless, there are Christians who continue to act in ways that prove faith's unwillingness to let the ship sink.[10]

Pastoral Reflection: The Dissonance Between Faith and Deeds

A compelling historical illustration of the tension between professed faith and lived deeds can be found in Abraham Lincoln's Second Inaugural Address. Notably, Dr. Louis Warren, Chancellor of the University of Oxford during Lincoln's era, observed "267 of the 702 words were direct quotations from the Bible and words of application made to them."[11] This remarkable incorporation of Scripture was not merely rhetorical flourish; it emerged naturally from Lincoln's devout Christian faith, which profoundly shaped his governance and instilled in him a strong sense of accountability before God. This accountability was nurtured through the close pastoral guidance of Reverend Phineas Gurley.[12]

Following the delivery of his address, Lincoln penned a short letter expressing gratitude to Thurlow Weed, a friend (often kept at arm's length) and newspaper publisher who praised the speech.[13] The tone and content of Lincoln's reply are revealing, especially in how he articulates the public's mixed reception to his address. Lincoln opened the letter candidly, writing, "Everyone likes a compliment,"[14] but quickly tempered this observation with a sobering reflection:

> I believe [the inaugural address] is not immediately popular. Men are not flattered by being shown that there has been a difference of purpose between the Almighty and them.[15]

In one sense, Lincoln's point requires minimal analysis. He articulated an easily observable truth: While people universally enjoy affirmation of their virtues, they generally recoil when confronted with the reality of their faults—particularly when those faults place them on the wrong side of divine righteousness. Lincoln understood this response as inherent to humanity's sinful nature, an insight compelling him to address the discomfort directly.

Even though Lincoln knew he spoke primarily to an audience composed of God-fearing Christian citizens, he felt compelled to deliver this challenging truth openly. The reason for this was clear: Believers, who profess faith in alignment with God's will, paradoxically often find it most difficult to accept correction when they deviate from that path. Yet, as Lincoln implicitly recognized, these uncomfortable truths are precisely those which believers, above all others, must be willing to hear and heed.

Lincoln took a bold and necessary risk by confronting his audience with this very accusation. In the speech, he directly addressed the irony faced by a divided nation, composed largely of people who "read the same Bible, and pray to the same God, and each invokes His aid against the other."[16] Lincoln posed a penetrating rhetorical question: Should either side genuinely expect God to be in conflict with Himself? He answered unequivocally, asserting, "The prayers of both could not be answered."[17] To reinforce this logic, he further questioned, "Shall we discern therein any departure from those divine attributes which the believers in a living God always ascribe to Him?"[18]

The answer, of course, is emphatically no. Scripture affirms repeatedly God is immutable (Num. 23:19; Mal. 3:6; 1 Sam. 15:29; Isa. 46:9–11; Ezek. 24:14; James 1:17; Heb. 13:8). He does not change, nor does He act in contradiction to His divine nature. Consequently, He cannot simultaneously endorse and oppose the same action or belief.

Lincoln's theological reasoning underscored an uncomfortable truth: Those seeking outcomes contrary to God's holy will should not anticipate His blessing but rather expect His resistance and correction. Demonstrating his careful theological consideration, Lincoln referenced the sobering words of Jesus recorded in Matthew 18:7, implicitly suggesting the horrific reality of the Civil War was a form of divine judgment against those responsible for perpetuating the moral evil of slavery. Importantly, his indictment extended beyond the obvious guilt of the South to include the complicity of the North, where silence and inaction allowed slavery's continuance for far too long. Ultimately, Lincoln acknowledged a shared national guilt—a responsibility in which he humbly included himself.

Building on Lincoln's reflections, another significant insight emerges—one many people, even devout believers, hesitate to acknowledge openly: God indeed chooses sides. This statement must be understood carefully. It does not imply trivialities, such as God favoring a particular sports team (Rom. 2:11), nor does it suggest the troubling doctrine of Double Predestination, where God arbitrarily selects some for salvation and others for condemnation. When it comes to humanity's rescue from sin, death, and Satan, Scripture plainly declares God desires salvation for all (John 3:16–17; 1 Tim. 2:4; 2 Pet. 3:9; Ezek. 18:23; Matt. 23:37).

Rather, the point here is both simple and profound: God stands unequivocally opposed to evil.

This foundational truth appears consistently throughout Scripture. It is repeatedly illustrated in the Old Testament narratives, each of which conveys not only God's clear opposition to evil but also His expectation for His people to align themselves similarly (Ps. 1:6; Josh. 24:14–15; Deut. 30:15–20). This theme of divine allegiance carries seamlessly into the New Testament, exemplified vividly in the ministry of Jesus. For instance, Jesus explicitly chooses sides in matters such as divorce (Matt. 5:32 and 19:9), clearly takes the side of the woman threatened with stoning by the Pharisees (John 8:1–11), and plainly asserts, "Whoever is not with me is against me" (Matt. 12:30). Additionally, in Luke 11:28, Jesus underscores the blessedness of those who align themselves with God's Word, emphasizing the necessity of hearing it and steadfastly holding it as the foundation of salvation.

Paul further reinforces this principle. By divine inspiration, he famously proclaims, "If God is for us, who can be against us?" (Rom. 8:31). Even more pointedly, Paul addresses a divided congregation in Corinth regarding the proper observance of the Lord's Supper. He acknowledges the existence of divisions within the church, writing:

> For, in the first place, when you come together as a church, I hear that there are divisions among you. And I believe it in part, for there must be factions among you in order that those who are genuine among you may be recognized. (1 Cor. 11:18–19)

The Greek term Paul uses here for "genuine" is δόκιμοι, which carries the sense of being "approved" or "judged worthy." But judged by whom? Clearly, by God. In stating this, Paul is making explicit that God actively distinguishes between right and wrong positions, affirming one side and rejecting the other. In other words, God chooses a side.

Returning to Lincoln, the stinging force of his message derived from his willingness to expose evil carefully concealed beneath layers of apparent righteousness. Another layer of discomfort emerges when acknowledging how many individuals are indifferent to moral clarity—what matters most to them is that nothing disturbs their personal interests. The contemporary debate around abortion highlights this vividly. For example, it is all too common to hear a Christian say, "Sure, abortion is terrible, and I'd never choose it for myself. But I don't think it's right to restrict someone else's right to choose one."

Such a position, however popular, stands directly opposed to the moral clarity revealed by God. If someone holds to this perspective, they must face the uncomfortable realization God is not aligned with them.

Lincoln courageously communicated precisely these uncomfortable truths, fully aware—as he confided to Weed—his message would be unpopular. He concluded his letter by succinctly encapsulating the gravity of denying moral clarity:

> To deny [the difference in purpose between God and evil], however, in this case, is to deny that there is a God governing the world. It is a truth which I thought needed to be told, and, as whatever humiliation there is in it falls directly on myself, I thought others might afford for me to tell it.[19]

Lincoln's words remain profoundly relevant. When someone persists stubbornly in a wrong position, rejecting even the possibility of correction, they implicitly challenge the very idea God is governing justly. To claim one's own moral superiority over God's revealed will does not merely signify a theological disagreement; it approaches the denial of God's authority, and perhaps His existence altogether. Both possibilities represent the gravest affront.

Admittedly, no one enjoys receiving correction, especially when it concerns matters of faithfulness to God's will. Nevertheless, such correction, piercing as it may be, represents an essential aspect of God's kindness. The penitent believer, transformed by the Gospel, learns to receive these warnings not as judgments of condemnation but as gracious invitations back into alignment with God's goodness and truth.

Thankfully, Lincoln possessed this clarity, boldly articulating truths others hesitated to voice. Consider the transformative potential if more public figures displayed similar courage—calling sin precisely what it is and affirming Christ as the singular source of rescue and redemption. Imagine a society whose people still possessed ears attuned to such a vital message.

Yet courage alone is insufficient if it is not anchored in substance. The Church must not only choose sides. It must have a firm footing. Without doctrinal stability, moral courage drifts into sentimentalism. And where sentiment leads, confusion follows.

Chapter 6

The Substance of Resistance

To stand firm first requires something substantial to stand upon. Many would say the contemporary Church is its worst enemy in this regard, lacking any real substance, ultimately rendering itself a rudderless vessel. Matt Walsh considers contemporary Christianity to be little more than self-help inspirational platitudes devoid of sacredness and reverence, entirely intent on selling the Gospel apart from distinguishable doctrinal or biblical boundaries.[1]

This is to say Christianity is currently embracing what Luther referred to as the theology of glory, as opposed to the better theology of the cross. Commenting on these spheres, Gerhard O. Forde insists a theologian of glory can only end "by calling evil good and good evil," while a theologian of the cross can "say what a thing is."[2] Forde lifts these words directly from Martin Luther's *Heidelberg Theses*, namely, thesis 21.[3]

Walsh argues, without the theology of the cross, the Church will continue to perpetuate its own impotence. Moreover, a faith tradition lacking cruciform theology while failing to catechize its children according to the Gospel's doctrinal boundaries will lose its forthcoming generations. Walsh believes such catechesis will equip children for transmitting truth's torch to those who follow.[4] Indeed, substance is required for this. If a child does not learn the doctrines of faith, he or she will not be able to stand firm against external forces seeking to undermine them, and truth's flame will be extinguished.

This is not merely an issue of generational inheritance. It is theological necessity. As the previous chapter explored, God chooses sides. He does not bless half-hearted allegiances or moral compromise. But to stand on God's side requires knowing what that side is. That knowledge is doctrinal. It is taught, confessed, and practiced. Without such clarity, the Church cannot distinguish between faithfulness and betrayal. Moral courage is impossible without theological conviction.

Professor of Biblical and Religious studies at Grove City College, Carl R. Trueman, agrees with Walsh, adding additional concern for maintaining Christianity's historical rites and ceremonies. For Trueman, a disconnect from the religious lives of those who came before disrespects the past, considering them an unworthy source of significant wisdom for the present.[5] This can only lead "to the rampant fragmentation and crass worldliness of the church herself."[6]

Trueman blames postmodern Protestantism's desire to reflect the culture rather than the Church's innate character demonstrated through longstanding liturgy and practice. He points to ever-sought megachurch aesthetics as proof "of the penetration of the anticulture."[7] Eric Metaxas agrees, considering such behaviors as little more than a demonstration of "religionless" Christianity.[8]

Neither Walsh's, Trueman's, nor Metaxas's concerns are lonely ones. In his book *No Reason to Hide: Standing for Christ in a Collapsing Culture*, award-winning author Erwin W. Lutzer considers the vital question: Is contemporary Christianity interpreting the culture through the Bible, or is the Bible being interpreted through the culture?[9] He argues the latter lens is employed for the most part.[10] Professor of Political Science at Seton Hall University, Jo Renee Formicola, believes even though such a process is dreadfully foolish, it is likely intentional. Formicola is convinced Vatican II deliberately attempted to dismiss the Church's substance to become more palatable to the culture.[11]

For her, the evidence is the Roman Catholic Church's steady loss of "civil and moral influence, especially in the West, due to demographic changes, increasingly secular shifts in public policy,"[12] and the ready embrace of more secularist agendas.[13] She measures the loss honestly, noting abortion, gay marriage, and so many other practices contrary to Roman Catholic doctrine are flourishing in places in Europe where Catholicism still retains authority or direct influence.[14]

Larry Golemon takes a somewhat nuanced view of the previous concerns, electing to include shallow intellectualism trends among pastors who prefer clergy to be seen as filling a corporate role rather than a form of moral authority. He offers that many prefer to compartmentalize pastoral ministry according to function (senior pastor, youth pastor, administrative pastor, and the like) rather than its symbolic or iconic identity. Golemon considers this "both ahistorical and unwise . . . as clergy inadvertently symbolize a community's ideals of spirituality, morality, and sacred knowledge; so they bear a distinct responsibility to live in that role."[15]

Provost and research professor of theology at Grace Bible Theological Seminary, Owen Strachan, speaks in a parallel vein. In his volume *Christianity and Wokeness: How the Social Justice Movement Is Hijacking the Gospel—and the Way to Stop It*, Strachan suggests, "the church has not thought deeply" about the issues facing it.[16] Strachan announces almost emphatically, "Christianity is not hostile to deep thinking; Christianity is grounded in it."[17]

In her volume *How the West Really Lost God*, well-respected intellectualist Mary Eberstadt seems somewhat disinterested in the more acute notions mentioned above. Eberstadt elects to paint a wide-sweeping image less inclined toward indicting individuals based on substance but instead more so as entire societies turn away from religion for a multitude of interconnected reasons. Still, she admits the process is a tragic trading away of the Christian ethos for one rejecting Christian thinking entirely.[18]

Pastoral Reflection: Conviction or Conformity

This deterioration of substance and the ecclesial confusion it fosters became undeniably vivid during a 2022 religious liberty conference I attended. The three-day conference began with a strong affirmation of the Nicene Creed and an encouragement to unity around the essentials of faith. The conference's benefactor urged attendees to set aside denominational particulars for the sake of principled cooperation in the public square. It was a promising beginning.

Unfortunately, the event was dominated by mega-church pastors giving sermons that did, in fact, insist on acceptance of distinctly theological things—things about God laying this or that unprovable premise on the speaker's heart, pre/post-tribulation concerns, "deeds, not creeds" dogmatics, and a whole host of other rudderless theological ramblings particular to popular evangelical Christendom. Moreover, these same speakers went out of their way to take jabs at traditional churches. Lutheran, Roman Catholic, old-school Presbyterian, or old-guard Methodist—it didn't matter. If your church was inclined toward maintaining tradition and creeds, historic rites and ceremonies, you needed to get with the times. You needed to be courageous, to step out of conformity and get radical for Jesus.

The only one in the room wearing a clerical collar, I became a living target for their dismissals. And yet, I was not offended. I am joyfully guilty of believing tradition, rite, and creed safeguard truth. I firmly believe that the more a church seeks relevance through cultural conformity—rather than grounding itself in historic, doctrinal substance—the more irrelevant it becomes to a culture already skilled at devouring the shallow and malleable. I am convinced that without a grounding in historic, doctrinal substance, such churches are inherently incapable of resisting the cultural tides.

Amid the noise, one speaker stood out—Dr. James Lindsay, an agnostic, who offered the most incisive theological commentary of the entire conference.[19]

During his presentation, Lindsay referred to Brazilian philosopher and educator Paulo Freire, the father of Critical Pedagogy, as one of the truest originators of Critical Theory. As he did, he made a stinging observation. He noted that fundamental to Freire's position was the deconstruction of the traditional churches. Lest he offend his hosts outrightly, Lindsay implied Freire didn't appear concerned in his writings about the newer, more contemporary churches. These churches were already apart from what could shield their deeper connection to truth. They'd given it up voluntarily in their efforts to be found acceptable to the world rather than distinct from it. He inferred the framework of contemporary churches (whether they're willing to admit it or not) is primarily experiential—the manipulation of emotional highs and lows. He explained this as the best platform for replacing hard and fast truth with subjective sensitivity, namely, making what someone "feels" about truth the center of the experience.

Conversely, Lindsay sensed Freire's concern that traditional churches would naturally serve as fortresses against this strategy. Freire saw them as set apart from culture by objective boundaries. Their creeds hold the line on what is and is not true. Their traditions and worship practices are near-impenetrable expressions of those truths. It would seem in Freire's mind if Critical Pedagogy was going to help usher in a purer era of socialism, the traditional churches needed to be in the crosshairs of the effort's heaviest artillery. Tear down the traditional institutions and rebuild new ones. The contemporary churches have already proven themselves willing to follow along in stride, being shaped by their inherent desires for acceptability to the culture rather than expecting the culture to conform to the truths they hold dear.

In summary, Lindsay's two-fold warning was clear. First, Christians should take note that one of Critical Theory's most influential proprietors believed traditional churches were likely a society's last line of defense against Marxist pedagogies. Second, the more a church abandons substance for experience, the more it invites its own deconstruction.

Lindsay's remarks warranted more than applause—they demanded further reflection. After the session, I managed to speak with him. The conversation clarified what the conference, for all its energy, failed to grasp: genuine courage in the Church arises not from enthusiasm but from conviction rooted in truth. It is not emotionalism that builds fortitude but substance. And where that substance is missing, courage gives way to foolishness masked in zeal.

Our brief discussion ended with an invitation for Lindsay to speak at the next year's conference I host in Michigan. He accepted. True to his word, he returned and did not disappoint, delivering a compelling presentation on Marxism's gnostic roots. That evening, over a shared appreciation for fine whisky, we continued the conversation in my home. As we sipped and talked, Lindsay returned to a question he raised earlier: Why do so many traditional, conservative churches—those most doctrinally prepared—remain on the sidelines in the cultural moment that arguably demands their leadership?

I told him there are many reasons, but one in particular stands out. Even as these churches have remained committed to their confessions, certain components of their theology have atrophied for lack of use. Chief among them is the doctrine of the Two Kingdoms—a distinctly Lutheran contribution, later echoed by the American Founders, which provides a framework for understanding the Christian's role in both the Church and civil society. Where this theology is forgotten or misapplied, engagement wanes. And where engagement wanes, confusion rushes in.

That concern wasn't theoretical. It surfaced again in my own denomination the next year.

Ahead of the 2024 presidential election, a letter was circulated by a district president within my own denomination. It urged pastors to be cautious when addressing political issues. The letter's tone was pastoral—gentle, even—but its subtext was unmistakable. Topics such as abortion and human sexuality should be handled as matters of opinion, not doctrine. Pastors were warned against the risk of offending the faithful. The message was clear: Silence is safer.

But this kind of reasoning forms the undertow carrying the Church into dangerous waters of abdication. Regardless of the topic the culture might claim for itself, Christ is Lord over all. And because His reign extends to every corner of human existence, all things require Christological measurement.

Therefore, Christians go into the fray. They go because, as the body of Christ, they belong everywhere, not just in the pews. But they do not go alone into the public square. They are led. Faithful pastors go on behalf of and alongside the flock entrusted to them. When they engage, they model what the whole Church is called to be: a visible, vocal presence in the world for the sake of the truth.

Which is why I offer this word to the faithful: If your pastor is engaging these issues—not carelessly, but courageously—pray for him. Encourage him. Stand beside him. His burden is not light. He will be accosted on the phone. He will receive anonymous letters and accusatory emails. He will lose church members, and as such, will lose friends. Some will walk away and say it was because he was divisive, political, or unloving.

But he is not. He is faithful.

In his faithfulness, he'll understand his congregation's aversion to conflict—the desire to avoid the messiness of controversy.

Nevertheless, remember your pastor is already in it. He is confronting what most people would rather ignore. He is doing what he can to protect you and your family from some very real monsters, some you can't always see. This is never safe.

And yet, this is the war zone. These are the trenches, and hell's bullets are flying.

Pray for your pastor. Then pray for the nerve to step in beside him—and go. And take heart: The faith once delivered to the saints is not lost. It forever remains a burning torch passed from generation to generation, safeguarded not by cultural favor but by conviction. When the Church stands firm in substance and truth, even the gates of hell cannot prevail against it. This is no less true now than it was in the days of the apostles, the Reformers, or Lincoln. Stand firm. Stand faithful. And others will follow your light.

That said, if the Church recovers its substance, what follows will not be worldly praise—but persecution. Substance brings clarity. Clarity invites hatred. Hatred is an uncomfortable consequence. But relative to faithfulness, it is a holy one.

Chapter 7

A Church Worth Hating

Matt Walsh insists substantive religion inherently produces more than superficial introspection or the nonchalant handling of challenges. Instead, "reverent faith is militant, aggressive,"[1] and the exhortation by its leaders must include demands for action, often resulting in personal sacrifice.[2]

Walsh's point is important. Describing Christianity using historical terms, noting the distinction between the Church militant and the Church triumphant,[3] Walsh reminds readers the Church on earth is called militant for a reason. It is mindful of its substance and deliberate in its action. Simply put, its goal is the extension of Christ's kingdom amid a world trapped in sin.[4] As the Church moves, it meets with the world, administering the Gospel antidote for despair and fear. In this effort, a struggle ensues, and suffering is endured, but these hardships are worth the reward.[5]

Michael Conway reflects a similar premeditation, writing that the Church must carry itself in two directions. The first concerns substance, or "the church's tradition and self-understanding."[6] The second he calls crucial, namely, "outwards to the ambient world and culture."[7] For Conway, the Church's substance is necessary for salvation and cultural alteration.

Frederica Mathewes-Green wonders if Christianity has already passed the point of no return relative to cultural influence. And yet, she wonders aloud if what happened in ages past might happen again. She writes, "We can practice our convictions and support each other, but that's a long way from changing the culture. Are we fated to live in a time when Christians are becoming more and more irrelevant in the public arena? All the early Christians could do was die. But they did that with such grace that they gradually drew the whole world to Jesus Christ."[8]

Erwin Lutzer carries the banner of suffering further, contending that suffering "communicates the gospel in a new language."[9] In Lutzer's mind, not only are faith's fruits born from immovable conviction a demonstration of substance, but so is the resulting suffering. Moments requiring Christian courage and endurance to be demonstrated through suffering are powerfully influential for onlookers. Of course, Christ more than infers this by His words in Matthew's Gospel:

> "Blessed are you when people insult you, persecute you and falsely say all kinds of evil against you because of me. Rejoice and be glad, because great is your reward in heaven, for in the same way they persecuted the prophets who were before you. You are the salt of the earth. But if the salt loses its saltiness, how can it be made salty again? It is no longer good for anything, except to be thrown out and trampled underfoot. You are the light of the world. A town built on a hill cannot be hidden. Neither do people light a lamp and put it under a bowl. Instead they put it on its stand, and it gives light to everyone in the house. In the same way, let your light shine before others, that they may see your good deeds and glorify your Father in heaven." (Matt. 5:11–16 NIV)

James believes the same as what his brother and Lord preached in the Sermon on the Mount. He further describes Christian suffering not as detrimental to a believer's faith but as something capable of making an indwelling faith even sturdier. James writes: "Count it all joy, my brothers, when you meet trials of various kinds, for you know that the testing of your faith produces steadfastness. And let steadfastness have its full effect, that you may be perfect and complete, lacking in nothing" (James 1:2–4).

Relative to the Lord's words in Matthew 5:11–16, David P. Scaer, a foremost scholar on the Gospel of Matthew, upholds Walsh's juxtaposition of cost and reward, writing, "The persecution that the believers are undergoing is diametrically opposed in its outward appearance to what God will eventually do for them."[10] Further along, Scaer concludes plainly that a Gospel-built Church is a persecuted Church.[11] Processing this same information, while attempting to wrangle ungodly zealousness leading to Christianity's misrepresentation, Lutzer offers helpfully that even the persecuted Church embraces its persecutors in love. It does not shrink from engagement but understands humility and love as truth's best vehicle. "Truth and love," he writes, "are not enemies."[12] This point will be examined further in the section titled "Engagement in the Public Square as Mission."

Pastoral Reflection: The Comfortable Collapse of a Church Unhated

The Lord said, "Peace I leave with you" (John 14:27). But what does that peace look like in our time?

The *National Catholic Register* reported anti-Christian hate crimes are up 44 percent in a single year.[13] Open Door's *World Watch List* shared that more than 365 million Christians faced "high to extreme" levels of persecution in 2024. Today that number is around 380 million.[14] This means one in seven Christians has experienced excessive physical violence because of their faith. Nearly 5,000 of these cases resulted in death. Almost all of them happened in African and Asian countries.

Strangely, looking at the color-coded map, North America and Europe are grayed, indicating the kind of active persecution aimed at snuffing out faith entirely is nearly nonexistent. I wondered about this.

But not for long.

Apart from the proof that much of mainstream Christianity's doctrine is meme-generated, I once mentioned in an Easter sermon how countries like ours aren't exactly robust targets for the devil when it comes to battling faith. We've proven more than capable of dismantling it ourselves. A few examples:

In stride with its neighboring European countries, Scotland's parliament made misgendering someone a criminal offense punishable by up to seven years in jail.[15] It received vocal support from its churches. Across the Atlantic, Canada has endured similar ideological enforcement for years. Just south of its border, here in the United States, we're certainly not far behind. Christian pastors bless Planned Parenthood clinics, claiming Jesus was pro-choice while defending a mother's so-called right to kill her unborn child up to and after birth.[16]

I attended the 2024 State of the State address in Michigan. The invocator, a Christian pastor, spoke this way. Should I expect anything different? Just shy of 60 percent of Michigan's pew sitters elected state leaders who continue to make this infanticide possible.[17] These same leaders support children undergoing chemical castration and the criminalization of protesting parents. Add to that their targeting of Christian businesses and non-profit organizations for adhering to Christian doctrine.[18]

Still, so many American Christians yawn.

I also noted in the Easter sermon how President Joe Biden is proof the devil has little need to focus on us. As a self-described (in every sense of the word) devout Catholic, Biden went out of his way in 2024 to officially declare Easter Sunday was "Transgender Day of Visibility." Cardinal Wilton Gregory, the archbishop of the Archdiocese of Washington, D.C., called Biden a "cafeteria Catholic," meaning he picks and chooses what he wants to believe.[19] That could've been a zinging indictment if it didn't also apply to most of mainstream American Christendom.

Either way, I pushed back rather crisply from the pulpit. After the service, I was met with a visitor's venom, who insisted before an observing line of exiting worshippers that I was a bigot.

Unfortunately, this goes with the territory.

Still, I suppose I got off easy by comparison. Someone burned a trailer filled with Bibles in front of a church in Tennessee on that same Easter morning.[20] Unsurprisingly, for the most part, the news was hard to find. Although the progressives in my social media feed were sure to say things like, "Any church preaching hate should expect some level of backlash." And by "preaching hate," they mean anyone who doesn't believe as they believe when it comes to human sexuality, or worse, who publicly aligns with what the Bible teaches concerning sin, gender, life, and other topics.

Again, I wondered about America not making the persecution cut.

But only for a moment.

There's really no need to behead anyone for faith in Christ when the mouths on those heads couldn't tell you much about Him. For reference, watch for the annual social media posts from Christians claiming a connection between Easter and the ancient Babylonian festival of Ishtar. The ignorance in our churches of Christian history and its vernacular is absolutely astounding. But again, what should one expect from a Christianity learning its theology from the internet? What should one expect from a Christianity wanting to look and feel like the culture in almost every way, rather than being the holy body of Christ, distinct and set apart from the world?

To illustrate the point, imagine walking into a rock concert wearing jeans and a T-shirt. No one would care. But if I walked into that same concert wearing my alb, stole, and chasuble, people would likely notice—and be put off by it. The tragedy is many in the Church would be just as put off, preferring a pastor in concert attire to one visibly marked by sacred office.

But it's not only that the Church and the world are to be noticeably different. Our vocabulary is different too. We communicate using terms like *catechesis*, *Sanctus*, *Tenebrae*, *Kyrie*, *sacrament*, and *Agnus Dei*. Moreover, we move differently. We carry processional crucifixes. We bow our heads when the Lord's name is spoken. We do things like make the sign of the cross and sing sacred Scripture to one another. These practices are not merely traditional or aesthetic preferences. They are confessions in action—tangible expressions of doctrine.

Our liturgy catechizes. Our rites teach. Our language, movements, and even our architecture are intentional acts of resistance to cultural assimilation, marking us as Christ's own in a world preferring ambiguity over truth. We prefer church names never mistaken for nightclubs but instead teach what we believe—names like Holy Trinity, Redeemer, and Our Savior.

Side by side, the Church and the world look very little alike. Even further, the world isn't going to hate itself. It's going to hate what is apart from it. And it won't stand idly by when something is snatched from its grasp. Indeed, Christ said this, reminding His people: "If the world hates you, know that it has hated me before it hated you. If you were of the world, the world would love you as its own; but because you are not of the world, but I chose you out of the world, therefore the world hates you" (John 15:18–19).

This leads us back to the beginning: persecution.

Ann Landers once wrote to a reader, "Don't accept your dog's admiration as conclusive evidence that you are wonderful."[21] In other words, just because something affirms you doesn't mean you're right. Similarly, the absence of persecution doesn't necessarily signal spiritual health. It could just be the world is disinterested in paying attention to what it believes it already owns. Or, at the very least, it views American Christianity as a form of spirituality that can be easily adapted to its liking.

Maybe.

I suppose, in conclusion, the Lord did say, "Peace I leave with you." But that's not all He said. The complete text of John 14:27 is: "Peace I leave with you; my peace I give to you. Not as the world gives do I give to you. Let not your hearts be troubled, neither let them be afraid."

The Lord said this because He knew the Church on earth would exist perpetually in an unsettling time of oppression. Still, Jesus gives His believers peace. It's not the peace we might expect—as in the absence of conflict—but the kind that can endure persecution's fires, no matter how hot they get. It's also the kind of peace inevitably drawing the world's attention.

This is true because it tends to speak up even when doing so is dangerous.

By the power of the Holy Spirit at work for faith in Christ, believers have this peace. It settles a troubled heart and smothers fear, just as Jesus said. How could it not, especially when the One who promised it also conquered the last and most terrifying enemy, death? If not even death holds dominion over us, what else is there to fear? To labor for religious liberty, it is imperative to know the answer.

Moreover, it is important to know the peace of Christ's promises does not mean escape from conflict but endurance through it—and more, a clarity that sees opposition not as failure but as faithfulness rightly lived. Still, this opposition doesn't appear out of nowhere. It has context. It has a culture. The world's hatred of the Church is cultivated long before it strikes. It is nurtured by patterns of thought, societal norms, and redefinitions of virtue and vice. To recognize this, and to prepare for it, we must first understand the age in which we live.

Chapter 8

When Freedom Becomes a God

If the faithful Church is to be hated by the world, it is essential to understand what now defines that world. What cultural forces have so thoroughly reshaped the public mind that ancient Christian truths are no longer seen as noble but dangerous? The persecution facing Christians today—whether overt or subtle—is not happening in a vacuum. It is the fruit of an era unmoored from truth, community, and memory. The rise of secularism and radical individualism has not merely challenged Christian witness but rather has sought to replace it entirely.

Attentive to secularism's effects, Stanley Hauerwas and William H. Willimon offer clues relative to its influence on the Church as a community:

> The church need not feel caught between the false Niebuhrian dilemma of whether to be in or out of the world. . . . The church is not out of the world. There is no other place for the church to be than here. In the sixties, it became fashionable to speak of the need for the church to be "in" the world, serving the world. We think that we could argue that being in the world, serving the world, has never been a great problem for the church. Alas, our greatest tragedies occurred because the church was all too willing to serve the

> world. The church need not worry about whether to be in the world. The church's only concern is *how* to be in the world, in what form, for what purpose.[1]

Their point is as practical as it might seem for survival's sake to accommodate secularism, the Church cannot allow itself to be shaped by the culture. Doing so opens the Church and its people to identity and doctrinal confusion, leading to tragedies already demonstrated in history. They further place Nazi Germany as the definitive test for this theological mispositioning, describing the German Church as theologically ill-equipped against Hitler's forward momentum. For Hauerwas and Willimon, churches choosing secular acceptance above doctrinal faithfulness were found defenseless against Nazi assimilation. In other words, the Church was by no means the influencer but instead, the influenced.[2]

Hauerwas writes separately of secularism's attempt to influence Christianity's communal identity by developing "arrangements without memory,"[3] which is to establish extreme individualism or the standard no one in the community bears the same narrative but rather is free to choose his or her own story.[4] Willimon speaks similarly, acknowledging secularism's drive toward this community-exploding premise:

> [A]ll our talk of "freedom" is but the rattling of the chains binding us to the authoritarianism of a liberal, democratic culture, a culture that, whether it is intended to do so or not, destroys human community by fragmenting us into a herd of isolated units, each detached from tradition, community, history, and one another, all the while telling us that we are free. Ironically, in such a condition, detached from sources of true meaning, we have not gained our individuality but have lost it, for true individualism comes only from someone who knows and can name who she is.

> Of course, the democratic Empire now knows what the monarchs of old did not: detached, rootless, historyless individuals are more easily managed than people in groups, people who have names, stories, histories, and a home.[5]

Both Hauerwas and Willimon appear inclined to preserve the Church as a community built upon a common theological identity rooted in Christ for the purpose of navigating the world in which it lives. Timothy P. Carney agrees, describing America as "a land of opportunity because America is the land of civil society . . . to the extent that the American Dream of robust local community is alive."[6] Carney contends social networks born from community create a crucial sense of belonging that forms personal identities and a strong sense of purpose.[7] He comments, "The only way to maintain real and sincere closeness with a person is to entangle ourselves with that person through the bonds of institution—to live in community and to work toward common ends with that person."[8] He emphasizes the largest segment of American society, the middle class, needs a strong community for the sake of long-term stability, and when it comes to arenas beyond work and home, the Church is the community's most accessible form.[9]

Carl R. Trueman completely agrees with Carney, adding concern for the Church community relative to identity preservation, stating the Church must "be a community. If the struggle for Christianity is the struggle for the nature of selfhood, then it is worth noting . . . that selves are socially constructed and only come to full self-consciousness in dialogue with other self-consciousnesses."[10]

By comparison, secularism interprets American ideals microcosmically, insisting individuals must be strictly divided from community standards to take full advantage of American freedom. Perhaps this was already being observed in early America.

An eighteenth-century observer, Frenchman J. Hector St. John de Crèvecœur, described his fellow Americans as no longer pressed by religious belief systems but instead self-interested and moving far from their monistic communal beginnings into social and religious pluralism.[11] He predicted the transformation would result in religion's complete disappearance.[12]

In *Healing Humanity: Confronting Our Moral Crisis*, Alfred Kentigern Siewers admits to this paradox, noting constitutionally, current legal trends lean toward "each individual's ability to pursue his or her identity."[13] In the same volume, Gaelan Gilbert clarifies, "Anything perceived as an attempt to keep someone from pursuing his or her choices is understood as an evil that must be opposed."[14]

Alongside Siewers and Gilbert, Bruce Seraphim Foltz considers these things to be little more than expressions of modern Gnosticism and its demands "to ensure autonomy from an oppressive world of sinister origin, the individual must be self-defined."[15] Natasha Crain vocalizes radical individualism as secularism's bridge to humankind, stating a "major reason secularism is so influential is that it appeals directly to the desires of our fallen nature—it reinforces the desired authority of the self. . . . Your happiness is of utmost importance, and only you can decide what will make you happy—you're the boss."[16]

David Seckler defines radical individualism, clarifying it "asserts that all significant human behavior is choosing, purposive behavior. It is individualistic because it contends that all institutions or 'social collectives' can be explained in terms of the behavior of individuals alone."[17]

Paul D. Bush observes Seckler's definition, adding, "The 'alone' in the last sentence is absolutely definitive and demarks what appears to be an unbridgeable chasm."[18] Carl R. Trueman shows concern for radical individualism "as the specific and perhaps most obvious social manifestation of a much deeper and wider revolution in the understanding of what it means to be a self."[19]

Speaking to the principle's *praxis* and *telos*, Roderick T. Long explains:

> [R]adical individualists tend *inter alia* to be motivational individualists, both in the "methodologically subjectivist" sense of explaining people's actions in terms of their beliefs, desires, and preferences, and in the "ethically internalist" sense of denying that there could be moral duties that did not somehow engage the agent's preferences. Indeed, most of these thinkers go beyond mere internalism to ethical eudaimonism [happiness, wellbeing], insisting that all moral duties must be in the agent's self-interest.[20]

Trueman nods to this compartmentalization, noting Thomas Aquinas demonstrated a similar separation of teleological understanding within human nature.[21] Perhaps humorously, like Siewers, Erwin Lutzer observes another paradox: Radical individualists collectively demonize community. In other words, radical individualism is self-indicting as an ideological community pit against the ideologies of another community. Frederica Mathewes-Green would have her readers remember the converse problem inherent to this verity: When one becomes free from obligation to others, those same others are free from obligation to you.[22]

In short, many cultural observers view radical individualism as unfettered narcissism seeing no need for community. As such, it provides a destructive platform for individuals to do, say, and be whatever they want beneath freedom's banner and without any definitive consequence shaped by stabilizing communal standards.

Michael Mascolo appears to agree with this position. Drawing attention to the narrowing of moral frameworks, Mascolo associates the constricting with "insufficient communal accountability."[23] Daniel Cox does the same, pointing to the Church's demonstrable disconnect from the public square as a fruit of community dissolution. Cox considers the Church an essential conduit into the civil sphere, noting when its community declines, so goes its levels of social and political engagement.[24]

These voices are not lonely. Timothy P. Carney uses a wide-angle lens to observe, showing how increased secularization resulting in radically individualized behavior creates hyper-individualized relationships in every aspect of society.[25] For example, he cites the "Gig Economy,"[26] framing it as a capitalist system in which "no entangling alliances or permanent commitments"[27] are made, resulting in a world where corporate communities no longer exist and "where workers are available when needed."[28]

Michael Conway counts radical individualism as the societal standard becoming most comfortable for many, saying plainly, "Individual persons now freely choose and construct the norm that will guide life, relationship, and religiosity."[29] This happens apart from communal bindings.

For Conway, radical individualism's theological implications are devastating. His point: Radical individualism convinces that as long as one is true to self, the divine will approve, guaranteeing one's blissful afterlife.[30] Describing the tendency to believe that "what matters is that I speak my truth," Jeff Myers acknowledges the "'no-judgment-allowed' mindset is growing in popularity among Christians."[31] As a result, churches are exchanging their Christological identities for the truthless philosophies of Sophism, Deflationism, Pluralism, and Pragmatism.[32]

However, Myers continues insisting for Christians, objective truth is sourced in Christ and can be known. And yet, those "who believe Truth can be known do not claim to know all of what is true. Rather, they argue that what we can know may be truly known."[33] He adds, no matter a person's acceptance or rejection of objectively true things, truth itself will always rise to the surface. This is demonstrated simply by things and ideas having knowable meanings, words being communicative, humans making rational arguments, and the discernible difference between facts and opinions demonstrated throughout human history.[34]

Pastoral Reflection: A Nation Adrift

Since the mid-twentieth century, America has increasingly come to see itself as a nation of orphans, lacking a shared narrative rooted in a paternal tradition. Dennis Prager noted to me in passing, "The melting pot is dead." His point was America no longer owns a unified culture but fragmented pockets of communities and nations, each with its own flag and little sense of collective identity. He went on to point out Flag Day is now marked in many school systems, not as a celebration of the American flag, but as a day for children to bring the flags of their ancestral homelands. This shift reflects a broader transition away from a coherent American identity toward a celebration of subjective truths, where the only absolute is the claim that no absolute truth exists.

Truth, in this cultural framework, becomes whatever one wants it to be. A man in New Mexico marries his computer.[35] Others seek licenses to marry their pets.[36] Gender, once understood as a biological given, is now treated as a self-defined category, leading to policies like the inclusion of girls in Boy Scout troops.[37]

This is modern America, where radical individualism reigns—where the freedom to be, do, say, and live as one pleases is prized above any shared moral compass. In the process, the nation's Judeo-Christian heritage has been systematically marginalized. Given the steady rise in religious liberty infringements, one could argue it is on a path toward eventual criminalization.

Christian judges have been removed from the bench, and Christian business owners have been fined beyond their capacity to remain in business. We are witnessing the results of governance rooted in freedom without objective truth, like a ship set adrift, rudderless, upon the unpredictable waves of postmodern secularism.

This outcome is difficult to refute. Consider it in light of the oft-invoked phrase, "life, liberty, and the pursuit of happiness." What is "life" without an objective starting point? President Obama once admitted that determining when life begins was "above [his] pay grade." If even a president declines to answer, can the citizenry be expected to know?

"Life" becomes whatever one says it is. "Liberty" may become the means by which one enforces their version of life, even at the expense of others, including the unborn. And "happiness"? It becomes whatever pleases the self, even if that means abandoning one's family to assume a new identity, such as that of a six-year-old girl.[38] All of this is now defended as a constitutional right—to pursue life, liberty, and happiness—detached from natural law and the enduring moral claims of biblical Christianity.

If this is what our nation's documents have become, then "life, liberty, and the pursuit of happiness" risks being reduced to a shield for the darkest human impulses.

But history presents a different picture. In 1854, the U.S. House Judiciary Committee declared:

> Had the people, during the Revolution, had a suspicion of any attempt to war against Christianity, that Revolution would have been strangled in its cradle. . . . In this age, there can be no substitute for Christianity. . . . That was the religion of the founders of the republic, and they expected it to remain the religion of their descendants.[39]

Despite modern efforts to reinterpret or obscure this heritage, the historical record remains clear. The Founders believed in Christianity's foundational role, spoke openly about it, and encountered little resistance, even from those among them who leaned toward Deism.

Elias Boudinot, a framer of the Bill of Rights and the first attorney admitted to the Supreme Court bar, captured this conviction:

> Let us enter on this important business under the idea that we are Christians on whom the eyes of the world are now turned. . . . Let us earnestly call and beseech Him, for Christ's sake, to preside in our councils. . . . We can only depend on the all-powerful influence of the Spirit of God, whose divine aid and assistance it becomes us as a Christian people most devoutly to implore.[40]

To understand the nation's founding documents as possessing a Christological foundation is essential to interpreting and applying them faithfully. So long as this understanding is preserved, these documents retain their noblest identity and legitimate authority. Without it, there are no meaningful boundaries to the "freedoms" citizens may demand, some of which will inevitably infringe on the freedoms of others. Left unmoored from this foundation, the documents become vulnerable to distortion, abuse, and, eventually, abolishment.

A product of the American Revolution and the father of American geography, Jedediah Morse, warned of this very pattern:

> In proportion as the genuine effects of Christianity are diminished in any nation, either through unbelief, or the corruption of its doctrines, or the neglect of its institutions; in the same proportion will the people

> of that nation recede from the blessings of genuine freedom, and approximate the miseries of complete despotism. . . . Whenever the pillars of Christianity shall be overthrown, our present republican forms of government, and all the blessings which flow from them, must fall with them.[41]

Morse's foresight echoed on June 28, 2006, when a future president of the United States, Barack Obama, stated with certainty, "Whatever we once were, we're no longer a Christian nation."[42] While the statement acknowledged America's religious diversity and affirmed freedom of conscience, it also revealed a profound philosophical shift. The language implied the nation once identified as Christian in character and that its founding documents bore that influence. But by calling it "whatever we once were," Obama relegated the nation's Christian heritage to the realm of bygone mythology. Whether or not intended, the statement suggested this legacy was no longer foundational—and perhaps no longer relevant.

In that moment, a deeper truth was exposed: Objective truth has been displaced by subjective interpretation, and the moral center of the Constitution may already be critically wounded.

The appropriate response is not withdrawal but engagement. For Christians in particular, the moment calls for clergy leadership—servants of Christ and His Church who are willing to reclaim their historic roles in shaping public life. The example is clear: Backus, Kirkland, Carroll, Spencer, Witherspoon, Muhlenberg—clergymen who not only ministered to their congregations but engaged actively in civic life. They cooperated in externals across denominational lines, ran for office, helped draft founding documents, and built lasting institutions. And when necessary, they resisted efforts to redefine religious liberty as anything but the freedom to private belief. They understood true religious liberty encompasses the right to proclaim truth publicly, to teach it, to live it, and to protect the conditions allowing the Gospel to be preached freely without fear of government reprisal.

The stakes are unmistakable. The choice before today's believers is equally so: to engage actively in preserving the foundations that make religious liberty possible or to passively accept its continued erosion toward extinction.

If freedom is to remain guided by truth, then the Church must not shrink from its public responsibilities. Yet such guidance cannot materialize apart from those ordained to provide it. As the culture descends into deeper confusion, the role of the clergy becomes more critical than ever. But is the Church's leadership ready to speak? Or has it too been silenced by fear and fractured by compromise? This question leads us to the pressing crisis within the pastoral vocation.

Chapter 9

When the Church Is in the Way

If the effects of secularism and radical individualism are as pervasive as we've seen, then the Church's response—particularly through its clergy—warrants honest scrutiny. Indeed, if the Church is increasingly sidelined, we must wonder whether its shepherds have stepped aside.

Relative to radical individualism's effect on clergy, Eric Metaxas has much to say. In particular, he shows concern for American pastors' marginal familiarity with Two Kingdoms theology combined with an unnecessary fear of the Johnson Amendment.[1] Concerning the Two Kingdoms doctrine (which will be extrapolated in a later section), they do not know how and why the right-hand kingdom might meet with or be necessary to the left-hand kingdom.

About the Johnson Amendment, they fear being labeled too political by government entities, often suppressing fears with the "it will never happen" mentality while simultaneously using church polity to stay comfortably protected from the demand for engagement.[2] Metaxas speaks of a spiral into silence keeping the pastor and his congregation apart from their place in civic engagement and its subsequent realities.[3] He also notes one of the pastors' grandest fears: congregations divided. He does this by comparing the same anxieties demonstrated among the churches in 1930s Germany.[4]

Carl R. Trueman, Michael A. Conway, and Timothy P. Carney, much like Metaxas, prove mindful of the secular world's hostility toward churches. Trueman writes, "It is . . . increasingly clear that the idea of religious freedom is coming under hostile pressure in Western society and no longer enjoys the status of an unequivocal good in the broader social imaginary."[5]

Michael Conway adds, "There has been an enormous shift in our culture, where religion has gone from being centre stage to being marginal or at least a limited player in terms of society at large."[6] Considered from the current angle, there is the fear of using one's religious liberty to preach about issues that, in today's society, will now be interpreted secularly and, as a result, be counted as bigotry.

This is to say what once was is now a distant and alien land and they do things differently there than they do in post-modern America. If a pastor wants to protect his church, he will tread lightly, necessarily keeping quiet. Carney expounds secularly-minded institutions are actively partnering with an increasingly agreeable government to drive "religion into solely the private sphere—out of the civic square, out of the market-place, out of politics . . ."[7] Pastoral fearfulness is, therefore, not surprising.

Barna Group observed similar pastoral worries in a 2022 study including responses such as "feeling constrained by the ideological differences between congregants," "fear that portions of my sermon may be used against me or taken out of context," and "feeling pressured to address issues in society."[8] In a similar 2022 study testing pastoral burnout, "current political divisions" ranked third among the causes, with "the immense stress of the job" being first.[9]

In short, pastors appear fearful of negative reputational branding leading to social or governmental reprisal. Additionally, they fear general congregational disapproval, which is demonstrated through direct and inter-congregational conflict, which leads to shrinking attendance and tighter financial constraints.

Pastoral Reflection: A Cultural Collision

There is more than one reason for me to write this book. One in particular traces back to an event that occurred in Washington, D.C.—a moment, though unexpected, became a formative lesson in understanding the pastoral vocation in contemporary America.

It happened at the crosswalk on First Street Northeast, situated between the U.S. Supreme Court Building and the U.S. Capitol. As I approached the intersection, two men—lobbyists, as I would later learn—engaged me. I had not sought out a confrontation. It arose solely because I was wearing a clerical collar. In a sea of passersby, I stood out—easily identifiable as someone operating within a distinct moral framework and likely apart from prevailing cultural norms.

In the exchange that followed, my life trajectory changed.

Their assumptions were relatively clear. As a clergyman visibly aligned with tradition, I was presumed to be a defender of the Scriptures—a book they characterized as "incompatible with human dignity" and "in conflict with the fundamental rights of others." From their perspective, I was culpable for teaching what they dismissed as regressive, Bible-thumping ideology misleading Americans into placing their trust in a bigoted deity.

To them, I represented a backwater America that should either get out of the way or disappear altogether so the nation could finally move forward toward its truest destiny.

These were not fringe voices. These were influential figures with access to the ears of those charged with protecting your religious freedoms. What I learned that day has never left me. In many ways, it marked the beginning of a road leading me to many microphones—some friendly, some not.

The first and clearest lesson: The Church is in the way. These men said so explicitly. The problem wasn't politicians or policies—it was and is the Church. Their efforts cannot succeed unless the Church steps aside.

The second: Pastors must be engaged within the halls of government. This is not the time for passive observers. Those who stand in the stead and by the command of Christ must acknowledge that their responsibilities extend into the places where the rulers of this world operate. Not only because Scripture mandates prayer and intercession for those in authority, but because the relative safety of local ministry—particularly in quiet or rural settings—rests behind a cultural wall already splintering.

My understanding of these things, at that moment, was exposed as deficient. My practice of preaching the Gospel, administering the sacraments, and trusting "God will handle the rest" had, in fact, become a form of complicity. It allowed for the erosion of the very freedoms necessary to do those things. If such detachment continued, I realized it would lead inevitably to a Church in the shadows—a result, for the opposition, that is not accidental but essential.

There is more.

The cultural climate surrounding pastoral ministry in the United States has changed drastically. This is because more and more of the citizenry have been dechurched—absorbed by youth sports, distracted by leisure, dulled by apathy. Regular church attendance has become less of an expectation and more of a rarity. As a result, to even see a pastor in a clerical collar is to see an alien. Pastors have become strangers.

In recent history, pastors could move about their communities with relative ease and with minimal concern for their safety. They were known. They were respected. People tipped their hats in greeting. They were invited to give invocations at high school graduations. They were asked to pray before city council meetings.

That time is gone. Today, pastors risk harassment. They risk being sued. In some places, it is no longer unthinkable for a pastor to be cursed at, threatened, or even spat upon.

Interestingly, many Christians are inclined to respond, "That'll never happen in America." But it is happening.

Even apart from the horrific persecution occurring around the world, we must acknowledge Christian persecution is rising here at home. It is being fed by radical individualism cloaked in tolerance. As this grows, the Church's place in American life diminishes. Unfortunately, far too many pastors appear unconcerned, assuming others will take up the cause.

I read a social media post a few years ago from a former seminary professor who confessed he doesn't usually wade into political matters. But when he read Beto O'Rourke's remarks about revoking tax-exempt status from churches refusing to perform same-sex marriages,[10] he wrote something to the effect of, "I'm really mad about this and might become a political activist!"

My only response, very John McClain in nature: Welcome to the party, pal.

He trains seminarians. Isn't he supposed to know already the countless portions of God's Word urging us to be engaged in our communities and world, which to the honest reader is nothing short of urging Christians to be who they are in the unavoidable areas of life? The public square's ability to tax churches is one of these, and the professor just pointed it out. I think the deeper he delves into the discussion enraging him, the more it will reveal to him the public square is one of the most significant, unavoidable areas of life.

In fact, when speaking of existing in Kingdoms, it is the only other one, beside the Kingdom of God, ever really expounded upon for the biblical reader. And so naturally, knowing we are bound to such spheres, the Word of the Lord comes to us with countless texts saying things like, "Always strive to do what is good for each other and for everyone else" (1 Thess. 5:15 NIV);

or, "Whatever your hand finds to do, do it with all your might, for in the realm of the dead, where you are going, there is neither working nor planning nor knowledge nor wisdom" (Eccl. 9:10 NIV).

In other words, a person cannot fight the fight forever for everyone. Knowing this, discern and act while you still can.

As Christian pastors, professors, or parishioners, we are not custodians of an ethereal abstraction. Theology that truly saves must also take shape in the world. Doctrine must not die at the church doors, barely surviving the walk from pulpit to parking lot. The Church, empowered by the Holy Spirit, has the strength to engage meaningfully. Indeed, she is called to engage. The preservation of religious liberty cannot be achieved solely through thought. Thought becomes word, and word becomes deed.

As Jacob Bronowski said, "The world can only be grasped by action, not by contemplation. The hand is more important than the eye. . . . The hand is the cutting edge of the mind."[11] And as Shakespeare mused, "Action is eloquence."[12]

Having realized the Church is now seen as an obstacle to progress—and pastors are often too silent in the face of this cultural hostility—the natural question becomes: What does faithful response look like? For that, one need not look further than Christ, who taught love in action through one of His most powerful parables. The story of the Good Samaritan speaks with particular force to the apathy and passivity marking many, not all, among the modern clergy. It invites God's shepherds to stop walking past what is plainly dying and to apply the doctrine of love.

Some time ago, I wrote a piece critical of New York's abortion laws. However, my aim was to express disgust at the Church's silence throughout the legislative process. My essential question: "Where were you while the coal for this engine was being shoveled into the locomotive?" I opened with a quote from William Hazlitt. He wrote, "We never do anything well till we cease to think about the manner of doing it."[13] He continued, "Reason may play the critic, and correct certain errors afterward; but if we were to wait for its formal and absolute decisions . . . the world would stand still. Many stay for facts till it is too late to actually pronounce on the characters."[14]

Hazlitt's words function as a modern commentary aligning with the parable of the Good Samaritan (Luke 10:25–37). While the parable's central aim is to show humanity's inability to fulfill the Law and thus the need for grace, it also contains a vivid rebuke of inaction. Jesus selected characters who should have known what love required—clergy.

In summary, a man has been bludgeoned, robbed, and left for dead. His life hangs in the balance. A priest sees him but continues his trek. Why? Because he has priestly duties to fulfill. A Levite follows and does the same. Why? Because he has Levitical things to accomplish. Both pass by the dying man. Both choose to stay in their vocational lanes, assuming someone else will handle the situation.

Hazlitt's words capture the moment: We see the facts—"What a horrible situation"—and we judge the characters—"Whoever did this should be ashamed." But we pass by.

"I have a sermon to write. I have a Sunday school program to design. I have a budget meeting for our church's school to attend."

Never mind the man in the road will never hear the sermon. Never mind aborted babies will never sit in your Sunday school classroom and benefit from your pedagogical prowess. Never mind Christian schools are being crushed into nonexistence under financial and ideological attack because those who could do something to stop it passed by, distracted.

"Preach and teach the Gospel! Administer the sacraments!" we cry. Yes, do that. But right now, for the sake of the Gospel's furtherance, help the dying man.

I have become convinced the Good Samaritan parable is the mandate for our age. This is true because it teaches genuine love. One might assume the opposite of love is hate. But it isn't. It's apathy. "I love you" finds its antithesis not in hostility, but in indifference. The apostle Paul insists, "Love is the fulfillment of the law" (Rom. 13:10 NIV). Love acts. To say this is to admit love moves God to wrath against wickedness. He judges because He cares. Love also drives Him to mercy, because He does not desire that any should perish. This love culminated in the greatest act of all: the sending of His Son, Jesus Christ, to satisfy divine justice, to die for the sins of the world, and to reconcile fallen humanity to God. He saw our need and He acted. He loved.

Empowered by this Gospel, we are equipped to love in the same way.

Once, while speaking at a conference, I posed a scenario for the listeners. Essentially, I said, "To any man in this crowd, I'd assume if your daughter was raped, I doubt very seriously that as you process the situation, you'll find yourself jumping straight to a softer, more churchly sense of saying, 'This is terribly unfortunate, and yet, God loves the rapist too, and so I just need to learn to forgive him and that's that.'"

I finished the point by insisting if any of the listeners were to be so careless, they must be judged as loveless. To act in love means seeking justice. Someone who loves would act to reestablish boundaries and, as best as possible, reclaim what was lost. A person who loves would engage against the forces he knows are actively seeking to dismember what is good and holy. He would seek and then stand for justice because he cares, not only for his daughter but also for ultimately making certain that the one offending, God willing, is countered and steered back to what is godly.

There will be time for preaching the Gospel of forgiveness to the offender, but until then, a boundary has been crossed and things must be set back in order.

Boundaries are being crossed. We must act. We must love.

Still, the faithful reclamation of the Church's public voice is not the burden of pastors alone. While shepherds must lead with clarity and conviction, they do so among sheep who are equally called to follow Christ with boldness. And so, the question naturally expands: If pastors must reengage, what of the people they serve? Has radical individualism so thoroughly permeated the pews that the Church is content to drift quietly into irrelevance? These questions demand consideration.

Chapter 10

THE WATCHFUL CHURCH

Just as radical individualism has weakened the resolve of many pastors, it has also dulled the courage of those they serve. The people in the pews—those entrusted with the daily living out of the Gospel—are increasingly content to compartmentalize their faith.

In a broad sense, Michael Conway points toward postmodern America's compartmentalization of life, writing how society has normalized keeping "apart our work lives, medical practice from church control, politics from religion, and so on. . . . There is a clear separation and differentiation of domains."[1] Conway supposes, as normal, the individual has the freedom to "choose and construct the norm that will guide life, relationship, and religiosity."[2]

Paola Pascual-Ferrá agrees, commenting, Christians are, by nature, "living more as an extension of the secular world today than as a distinct light to it."[3] Jeff Myers considers a Barna Group study proof of secularism's muscular grip. He writes, "Only 19 percent of churchgoing born-again Christians hold a biblical worldview. . . . The other eighty-one percent either are not aware of or disagree with core Christian doctrines about God, Jesus, the Bible, sin . . ."[4] He brings more disconcerting news, adding, "Fifty-one percent of Americans now say that the First Amendment . . . is outdated and should be rewritten to prevent hate speech."[5] He references Carl R. Trueman, who observed,

"Once harm and oppression are regarded as being primarily psychological categories, freedom of speech then becomes part of the problem, not the solution, because words become potential weapons."[6]

Two things are worthy of attention. First, by way of the Barna Group, Myers mentions the issue of ignorance as a factor. In other words, Christians can only navigate the issues as they understand them. If pastors are not teaching their people Christianity's relevance to public square issues, those same people will be incapable of navigating them authentically or successfully.

Second, by Trueman's First Amendment example, Myers highlights secularism's psychological influence on Christianity as a truth-proclaimer, resulting in self-sequestering and further compartmentalization. In this light, an important facet is revealed: the preservation and subsequent extension of the Gospel into the world.

Luther's Two Kingdoms doctrine has been mentioned superficially so far. Before a more thorough extrapolation in a forthcoming section, let it be known that at its center rests the preservation of religious liberty. Professor of Political Science at the University of Notre Dame, Daniel Philpott, insists the Church's efforts to preserve religious liberty are a consolidated demonstration of a universal human right, one well-cemented throughout history in court proceedings, political conventions, and national documents of governance.

For Philpott, if it is a human right, then it is also a fundamental right located within natural law.[7] Subsequently, the freedom to preach and teach the Gospel apart from interference or fear becomes something far more than doctrinal. It becomes materially human. Still, even apart from natural law, doctrinal consistency remains. Consider Paul's words to Timothy:

> First of all, then, I urge that supplications, prayers, intercessions, and thanksgivings be made for all people,

> for kings and all who are in high positions, that we may lead a peaceful and quiet life, godly and dignified in every way. This is good, and it is pleasing in the sight of God our Savior, who desires all people to be saved and to come to the knowledge of the truth. For there is one God, and there is one mediator between God and men, the man Christ Jesus, who gave himself as a ransom for all, which is the testimony given at the proper time. (1 Tim. 2:1–6)

Here, Paul instructs Christians to pray, intercede, and give thanks "for kings and all who are in high positions" of authority. These pleas concern the left-hand kingdom of civil rule. Paul explains the trajectory. His desire is born from God's Two Kingdoms framework, which maintains order so Christians "may lead a peaceful and quiet life, godly and dignified in every way."

Paul adds that such maintenance (also given prescriptively in Rom. 13:1–5) "is good, and it is pleasing in the sight of God our Savior," noting its innermost purpose: God's desire for "all people to be saved and to come to the knowledge of the truth." And what is this truth? The Gospel, which Paul defines: "For there is one God, and there is one mediator between God and men, the man Christ Jesus, who gave himself as a ransom for all . . ." Therefore, the goal of Christian engagement in the public square is to preserve religious liberty, which is the freedom to live in peace and quietness among one's neighbors while simultaneously enjoying the unhindered freedom to communicate the Gospel truth to all.

Erwin Lutzer agrees, eloquently describing Christianity's need to engage in cultural battles, not necessarily for the maintenance of natural rights but for the sake of "Christ, His gospel, and His cross. . . . The ultimate goal is to be a nation of Christians, and this can only take place through a faithful and courageous church sharing the gospel."[8]

As a side, Lutzer emphasizes the need for an individual's facts and ideologies to align.[9] A confused or disembodied Gospel is no Gospel. Metaxas agrees with Lutzer, except he does so by identifying the Gospel's incarnational nature. From Christianity's vantage, truth is a person, namely, Jesus Christ. To engage for truth is to preserve Christ's saving message.[10]

Natasha Crain shows great concern for protecting the Gospel in this sense, saying that to do so is to establish the only real ramparts protecting against deconversion, an increasingly popular method for communicating secular enlightenment designed to undermine faith. Crain posits examples of high-profile Christians falling away, only to use their platforms to draw others into the same skepticism.[11] Crain insists on crisply grasping the Gospel "for the sake of our own relationship with the Lord and for our ability to be a witness to others."[12]

Voddie T. Baucham Jr. argues for Gospel clarity relative to discerning falsehood. For example, he argues Critical Race Theory uses Gospel-familiar language yet completely opposes the Gospel's proclamation of forgiveness. Instead, CRT doles out forgiveness according to race, and it does so not considering salvation as freedom from sin through the real person and work of Jesus Christ but from imaginary oppressors conquered through social activism.[13]

Owen Strachan believes as Baucham, except he prefers to launch an all-out assault on social activism, considering it more than merely influential, but a complete commandeering of the Gospel. He writes, "Wokeness tweaks the doctrine of humanity, losing sight of the *imago Dei* as our constituent identity." He claims the social justice movement, as an extension of woke ideologies,[14] is inherently counter-Christian because it "foments the very sin it presumes to critique," cementing generational cycles of anger and victimhood. It approves evil actions as solutions to evil and destabilizes truth, making it narrative-driven rather than all-encompassing and absolute.[15]

Adjunct Professor of History at Concordia University in Chicago, Adam Francisco, agrees with Strachan's analysis that wokeness stands apart as incompatible with Christianity, except he adds the imperative for deliberate dialogue with the converse worldview. Dissecting wokeness's historical and current efforts, he believes it offers ample opportunities to Christians to confess Christ.[16]

Considering both the imposing magnitude and confusing nature of Christianity's opposition in America, it is no wonder Christianity is waning and its people remain disengaged. Having performed an informal survey among thousands of social media followers, Natasha Crain reports many Christians keep from sharing their faith in public because they fear rejection and retaliation for expressing culturally unacceptable positions. Fearful of the same, others confess feeling isolated by secular culture's high praise for strict individualism.[17] Further along, she observes other reasons, such as disagreement fatigue and the fear of cancellation. In summary, congregation members appear disengaged from the public square due primarily to theological ignorance, compartmentalized lives, ideological confusion, and fear of personal or reputational harm.

Pastoral Reflection: The Door Will Be Opened from the Outside

If the confrontation in Washington, D.C. noted in the previous chapter revealed the world's hostility to visible, traditional Christian conviction, then could it be tradition is a reliable instructor teaching the Church how to live amid such hostility with readiness, courage, and hope? Where the crosswalk exposed the reality that the discernible Church is an obstacle to progress, tradition reveals faithful endurance is not reactive but prepared. It does not lash out, nor does it retreat. It watches. It waits. It acts as it has learned. It does this in season, and it endures with expectation.

Perhaps we can consider this very point by way of the Church's traditional season of Advent.

For anyone familiar with the season, they know Advent's deepest intent is to assist the Christian for living within the tension of present darkness and promised light. It tempers boldness with humility, urgency with patience. Most of all, it readies the believer not only for Christ's return, but for faithful engagement in a world where freedom to confess Him is increasingly challenged. In this way, Advent serves not merely as a liturgical season but as a theological discipline for preserving religious liberty—not by force but by faithfulness.

Even for the Church—the divine collective of God's people endowed with better wisdom than the world—Advent remains a strange season. In a way, it's nearly dysphoric, understanding two entirely different moods simultaneously. This is to say, it's a profoundly penitential season and also wholly drenched in a strange joyfulness.

For one, the Church has its heart pitched with celebratory anticipation toward the Lord's arrival in Bethlehem. Advent anticipates Christmas, and believers are joyful because they know the moment of all moments happened there. God reached through the veil to rescue us. He didn't send an angel to do it. He didn't choose a champion from among us. He came and accomplished our redemption Himself. Aware of this, Advent bears an airy sense of cheer.

At the same time, Advent acknowledges the world's dreadful predicament. It knows sin, death, and Satan are real. And, even as it knows they've been defeated for all time by the Christ child of Bethlehem, still, Advent isn't so foolish as to think these specters won't try to do their worst to terrorize us until the Lord's return at the Last Day (Rev. 12:12).

And so, preparedness and endurance become Advent's undertow, carrying believers along in a better wisdom. Advent knows we remain wedged within this mortal frame's boundaries, while at the same time, we are citizens of another Kingdom—and that Kingdom will come. Every minute, its arrival draws closer (Rom. 13:11–12). Very soon, whether through a last breath or the Lord's glorious return, the door will be thrown open, and we will be with Jesus.

This brings something to mind. If anyone had a handle on this, it was Dietrich Bonhoeffer, the German Lutheran pastor imprisoned for his role in a plot against Hitler.

First, if you haven't read the Bonhoeffer compilation *Letters & Papers from Prison*, you should. It is, as its title describes, a collection of Bonhoeffer's communiqués written between 1943 and 1945 while imprisoned at Tegel Prison. It's incredibly enlightening and more than suitable for our modern societal climate. Second, within the anthology, you'll discover five letters scribbled between November 18 and November 23, 1943. Bonhoeffer wrote them to his friend Eberhard Bethge. Each letter is strangely plain, as though they could've been written from his desk at home. What makes them so bizarre to me is he speaks of prison life as if it were normal, as if this is what life is, and for us to expect anything different is silly. Considering he penned the letters at the end of November, mindful the Church would soon be immersed in Advent, he wrote near the beginning of the third letter, "Then comes Advent, with all its happy memories for us."[18] From there, he added: "Life in a prison cell may well be compared to Advent; one waits, hopes, and does this, that, or the other—things that are really of no consequence—the door is shut and can be opened only from the outside."[19]

After this, Advent isn't mentioned again. Instead, he goes on to other things, casually measuring each thought comfortably against phrases like "whether I'm freed or condemned."[20] In other words, Bonhoeffer not only sensed the season's deeper message, he was demonstrating it.

Christians perpetually live Advent lives. Whether free or condemned by this world, we go on.

Advent exists in real time, but it does so with a heart for the forthcoming time outside of time. It lives this way knowing human needfulness while also rejoicing the need of all needs has been met through the person and work of Jesus Christ. From there, it carries on, ever-awaiting mortal humanity's final moments, taking each day and its challenges as they come, fully aware anything and everything this dreadful world could ever aim at us has an expiration date. All of it is passing away.

Therefore, Advent reminds believers we are not inheritors of this transient world. We are inheritors of the world to come, a world without end. Soon enough, the door between these mortal and divine spheres will be thrown open, and we will experience the fullness of the freedom already ours right now in Christ.

Until then, we wait. We wade through the messes. These messes sometimes bring terrifying things. Still, death is the last and final enemy. But Advent's other trajectory—Christmas—assures us the One born in Bethlehem has already conquered and defanged this ultimate enemy.

The fourth and fifth of the November-tide letters from Bonhoeffer to Bethge were written on the same day. The fourth begins with an immediate, "Tonight's raid was not exactly pleasant…."[21] He was referring to an Allied Forces air raid that shook the prison. Bonhoeffer notes somewhat nonchalantly how surprised he was "to see how nervy the soldiers who had been at the front were while the alert was on."[22] His point was that the prison guards—former front-line soldiers—were overly anxious during the whole thing. From there, Bonhoeffer wanders back into casual discussion about a visit from his parents and the possibility of a forthcoming visit from Bethge on December 17. He concludes the letter a few short sentences later, but only after wondering so dryly if he'll actually make it to December 17.

He demonstrates so crisply he's ready to die.

But then he picks up his pen again, producing the fifth letter. The air raid still has him thinking. It was a surprise attack.

Of course, he wasn't scared. However, he was drawn back into Advent's mind.

Life is unpredictable. Readiness is important. Even more so is readiness for one's final hour of paramount consequence. And so, with his first sentence, Bonhoeffer's fifth letter insists, "It is only right that I should tell you briefly what arrangements I have made in case of my death."[23] After a couple of lawyerly sentences, using the same dryness as all the previous letters, he adds, "I hope that you will read this with your usual absence of sentimentality. It seems to me only reasonable to make the necessary provisions in case of such an eventuality."[24] He finishes with bequests to family and friends, followed by "So, that's it," and a brief word to keep the letter in a safe place.[25]

As with every human being in history, your final day is coming. Advent is a faithful friend who returns each year to remind us of the necessity for preparedness. Indeed, we don't know the day or the hour (Matt. 25:13), whether that moment is mortal death or the Lord's return. Either way, Advent comes along, giving us a friendly poke and saying, "Dear Christian, prepare your heart for the arriving Christ. He is coming, and nothing can stop Him."

As a pastor—as a fellow Christian awaiting the prison door's sudden opening—I share this brief excursus into Advent because I am convinced the season offers more than a personal call to spiritual readiness. It extends an ecclesial summons to public fidelity. The liberty we seek to preserve in the public square is not ultimately for comfort or cultural dominance but for proclamation—for the unshackled speaking of Christ crucified, risen, and returning. Bonhoeffer understood this. He knew, even in captivity, the Church's voice must not falter. He knew the Gospel's freedom does not depend on circumstance but is lived most clearly when circumstances press against it.

The Good Samaritan parable, explored earlier, does not only indict the pastor who walks past the dying man. It indicts all who see and do nothing. In this Advent-shaped life, the Church is called again to see clearly and act decisively. Whether clergy or lay, we are to step off the curb, bend low in mercy, and pour out what is needed, even at cost to ourselves. Faithfulness in this age does not look like preservation of comfort. It looks like interruption, compassion, and sacrifice. It looks like love in motion.

This is what religious liberty truly means: not the absence of struggle but the presence of resolve. Not withdrawal in fear but endurance in hope. To live an Advent-shaped life is to confess Christ in every season, trusting the doors of history, culture, and even death can be opened only from the outside—by the One who came once in Bethlehem and who is coming again in glory. Until then, the Church must not wait in silence. It must wait with courage, speaking clearly, enduring faithfully, and preparing the world to meet its King.

To wait with courage is to act with clarity, and has already been established, such clarity is only possible with sound doctrine. Having pointed toward the Church's public calling, we now pause to root this calling in the essential doctrine of the Two Kingdoms. This framework not only guards against confusion but equips the Christian for faithful engagement in both temporal and eternal realms, just as God intended.

☙

Section 2

Chapter 11

For the Welfare of the City

Before going any further, and since it has been mentioned more than once already, it is past time to provide contour to the Two Kingdoms doctrine. In summary, the doctrine specifies two spheres relative to God's governance. The doctrine's nomenclature speaks in terms of God's hands. The kingdom of the left hand is the kingdom of earthly rule. It is in this kingdom that God establishes civil governance for the sake of maintaining order and quelling chaos.[1] Erwin Lutzer rightly comments that God "delegates His authority to human beings in this kingdom."[2]

The kingdom of the right hand is spiritual. In this kingdom, the Gospel rules for the salvation of humanity.[3] The government does not rule in the right-hand kingdom. The Gospel does. Therefore, and as Eric Metaxas notes superbly, the government has no say in what is preached from Christian pulpits.[4] Equally, the Church does not rule in the left-hand kingdom. Although, it does have the freedom to engage in it as citizens, and perhaps more importantly, the responsibility to resist it when it forsakes its ordination by establishing and practicing evil. Concerning such things consider again the Lutherans, namely, the Magdeburg Confession of 1550, which historian G. R. Elton referred to as "the first full-blooded Protestant justification for rebellion and resistance."[5]

As the previous chapter emphasized, the Church's public engagement is not about cultural dominance but Gospel clarity and liberty. The Magdeburg Confessors understood this well. They prefaced their foundational document with three essential purposes. First, they restated what they considered unconquerable doctrines.[6] Second, they sought to prove religious liberty's essentiality and benefit—not merely as a political concern but as a theological imperative. When governments compel defection from the truth, they believed resistance was not rebellion but faithfulness.[7] Third, they warned against persecuting the Church, lest terrible consequences fall upon both body and soul.[8]

Of course, even as the text of Romans 13:1–5 is well-worn (and poorly handled) today, the Magdeburg Confessors experienced the same. In particular, Rome weaponized the text used following Luther's death to bring Germany into submission, and so the Confessors clarified:

> If God wanted superior magistrates who have become tyrants to be inviolable because of his ordinance [Romans 13] and commandment [The Fourth Commandment], how many impious and absurd things would follow from this? Chiefly it would follow that God, by his own ordinance and command, is strengthening, nay, honoring and abetting evil works, and is hindering, nay, destroying good works; that there are contraries in the nature of God Himself, and in this ordinance by which He has instituted the magistrate; that God is no less against his own ordinance than he is for the human race. All these things are most plain, nor can they be denied by anyone: If God has granted such great impunity to the greatest tyrant by His own ordinance and commandment, who will prevent him from laying waste all of nature, even if he could, and being innocent before God? Who will not provide his

> substance, his body, and even his life itself to the one who demands them for the occasions, ends, and nourishment of tyranny, because of the commandment of God? Who will do what is right contrary to the will of a tyrant, and be a survivor? Who will be left of all men as the only one doing right?[9]

An expert on Dietrich Bonhoeffer, historian Eric Metaxas observes similar handling of Romans 13 in 1930s Nazi Germany, writing, "The willingness of [German] Lutherans to keep the church out of the world reflected an unbiblical overemphasis on Romans 13:1–5."[10] In America, Lutherans were insisting quite the opposite. One such confessional Lutheran, Theodore Graebner, spoke candidly before the convention of the English District, Evangelical Lutheran Synod of Missouri, Ohio, and Other States, insisting the American Christian voter, as a "citizen in whom all political power ultimately resides . . . ought to consider himself an agency of God for righteousness."[11] Graebner insisted America's form of government made each citizen a ruler in the left-hand kingdom. Therefore, as both Christians and citizens, the Church held an organic role in civil affairs.

Eberhard Bethge, a close friend to Bonhoeffer, discovered an apparent gray area within a Two Kingdoms doctrine kept strictly divided by Romans 13. He writes:

> The levels of confession and of resistance could no longer be kept neatly apart. The escalating persecution of the Jews generated an increasingly intolerable situation. . . . We now realized that mere confession, no matter how courageous, inescapably meant complicity with the murders, even though there would always be new acts of refusing to be co-opted and even though we preach "Christ alone" Sunday after Sunday. During the whole time the Nazi state never considered it necessary to prohibit such preaching. Why should

> it? Thus we were approaching the borderline between confession and resistance; and if we did not cross this border, our confession was going to be no better than cooperation with criminals. And so it became clear where the problem lay for the Confessing Church: we were resisting by way of confession, but we were not confessing by way of resistance.[12]

Bonhoeffer would prove his grasp of the Two Kingdoms doctrine, insisting all earthly powers are by God's divine hand. Metaxas explains, "Governments are established by God for the preservation of order. The church had no fundamental quarrel with the state being the state."[13] Metaxas adds to this interpretation Bonhoeffer's position that the church must continually examine the state to test its legitimacy. Is it holding to its ordination and maintaining order for the good of the governed, or is its work leading to ungodly disorder and mayhem?

Bonhoeffer's point was, while the state has no right to dabble in the church's affairs, the church has every right to assist the state in preserving a godly heading. Therefore, the church must engage that it might also intervene and maintain.

Samuel Deressa observes Luther's agreement with Bonhoeffer: "For Luther, obedience does not always mean complete submission of the church to government authorities and/or a total withdrawal from politics, but rather a critical participation in politics."[14] He adds, "For Luther, the authority of temporal governments should be challenged when 'it cannot be obeyed without sin' (Acts 5:29), and when their actions contradict the purpose for which they are instituted."[15] Deressa understands Luther's words as broad-sweeping, necessarily avoiding the assertion that Acts 5:29 relates only to the Gospel's preservation. The Magdeburg Confessors understood Luther similarly, offering multiple biblical and early church examples of justifiable resistance throughout the Magdeburg Confession.[16]

Observing Luther's treatise entitled *Temporal Authority: To What Extent It Should Be Obeyed*, Volker Leppin affirms, "Luther is primarily concerned to set limits to temporal authority. That is already clear from the title given to the treatise. . . . This was a brave title for a text that had its origins in sermons that Luther preached in the presence of Duke John in October 1522 at Weimar."[17] Leppin adds firmly, "Only an extremely superficial reading of Luther can see him advocating a crass obedience to the authorities."[18]

In his book *A Time for Anger: The Myth of Neutrality*, Franky Schaeffer considers the sixteenth-century theologian William Perkins's words: "If it should fall out that men's laws be made of things evil, and forbidden by God, there is no bond at all: but contrariwise, men are bound in conscience not to obey."[19] Schaeffer continues by referring to the concepts found in the Bible as the standard measurement for judging a government's laws, thereby counting the Church as the government's divinely appointed overseer. Having already referred to America's forefathers as principally Christian, interestingly, Schaeffer feels inclined to assert this once more, noting they committed acts of civil disobedience relative to laws they considered abusive and counter to religious liberty.

The events leading up to the Boston Tea Party, which sounded echoes of governmental homage, serve as his example. Relevant, but admittedly dated, Schaeffer's view remains crisp to this day. In his study of church taxation, Assistant Professor of Law at Penn State University, Mark Storslee, reaches similar conclusions, referencing the Boston Tea Party while referring to James Madison's concern for even the slightest measure of governmental mandate concerning worship practice.[20]

The doctrine of the Two Kingdoms, properly understood, never grants Christians a license for passivity in the civil realm. Rather, it calls for discernment and courage—discerning when the state is acting within its divine ordination and when it has strayed, and then having the courage to respond faithfully. Resistance, when necessary, is not rebellion for rebellion's sake but a godly act of conscience against tyranny, as the Magdeburg Confessors, Bonhoeffer, and others have shown. This theological framework clarifies the Church's duty not only to proclaim the Gospel but also to serve as a guardian of righteousness within the civil sphere. To that end, the responsibilities of citizenship—especially in a nation like ours—are not incidental to Christian life but intimately connected to it. In light of this, I offer the following story.

Pastoral Reflection: Keeping the Republic

In the Advent posture of watchful readiness described previously, we learn that vigilance is not only for spiritual preparation but civic responsibility. Just as the Church prepares for Christ's return, the citizen must prepare for cultural and governmental shifts threatening liberty.

Milestones in a nation's life are worth reflecting upon, especially when they mark endurance in a world so often marked by upheaval. While many countries have seen shifting borders, rewritten charters, and evolving identities, the United States has experienced a remarkable degree of constitutional stability. Since its ratification in 1787, the U.S. Constitution has remained the governing framework of the nation for two and a half centuries—a rarity in global history.[21] By contrast, the average lifespan of most national constitutions hovers between twenty and thirty years.[22] Some nations, like France, have adopted numerous constitutions in that same period, replacing them every couple of decades.[23] Such contrasts underscore the extraordinary durability of America's founding documents and the exceptional continuity they have provided across generations.

For the most part, our nation's first president, George Washington, was an optimist. But relative to our Constitution, he was deeply aware that its success depended on the character and vigilance of the American people.[24]

Benjamin Franklin had similar concerns relative to the nation as a whole. Leaving the Constitutional Convention, he was asked, "Doctor, what have we got? A republic or a monarchy?"

"A republic," he so famously replied, "if you can keep it."[25]

In a way, I wonder if Franklin's response was somewhat rhetorical, ultimately assuming we'd lose what was given. I say this because few in our nation know or refer to the United States as a republic, even though we may pledge as much before our flag, saying, "and to the republic for which it stands." Most consider it a democracy, which it isn't. Perhaps worse, it seems more and more people, no matter which side of the ideological aisle they occupy, are slapping the label "A threat to democracy" on their political opponents. If by "threat to democracy" they mean pure democracy, then count me in. I'm happy to be a threat. And why? Because pure democracy is dangerous. Here's what I mean.

Democracies and republics are certainly similar in that elected officials represent each's citizens. In a democracy, governance emerges from the majority, ultimately resulting in near-unrestricted supremacy for the majority in all things. This means if the majority of citizens suddenly decided all houses in the nation must be painted blue, then the minority citizens who prefer red must comply. Now, take that to its absurd extent. When you do, a pure democracy means the minority exists in danger with every new law.

In a republic, minority positions are protected because laws can only be made as they align with the nation's governing charter. The American charter includes the U.S. Constitution and the Bill of Rights. These documents identify inalienable rights that cannot be infringed, no matter what the majority of citizens and their representatives might prefer. The documents establish boundaries that simply cannot be crossed.

Somewhere along the way, I learned another critical distinction between democracies and republics. I don't remember who said it, but the point was a citizen's only real job in a democracy is to vote. Beyond that, everything is as it is. Why? Because after the citizen chooses his representatives, those representatives become supreme. However, in a republic, the citizens hold ultimate authority, thereby making a citizen's duty a 365-day effort. In a republic, constant engagement beyond one's vote is the citizen's greatest responsibility.

Maybe that's why Franklin said what he did. "If you can keep it" assumes a citizen will embrace his greatest responsibility and engage. Participation is far harder than simply pulling the lever on election day and then wandering back to life, letting the government have it all. Engagement requires citizens to care, get involved, hold politicians accountable, and defend the nation's charter and the inalienable rights it commends. Such involvement requires serious commitment.

Commitment will inevitably become public. In other words, people will know a committed person's beliefs. Therefore, commitment requires courage, perseverance, resilience, the will to sacrifice, and so many more noble attributes that few in our day seem willing to exude for fear of being canceled by the opposition.

In the end, a republic of disengaged and uncommitted citizens is one destined to become little more than a memory.

Considering all this, a particular text comes to mind. In Jeremiah 29:7, the Lord prompts His people to engage wherever they live, mandating they serve for the welfare of the city in which they dwell. He expects their engagement because "in its welfare, you will find your welfare."

Another text comes to mind. Proverbs 14:34 reads, "Righteousness exalts a nation, but sin is a reproach to any people." The word used in the Hebrew for nation is גּוֹי. Essentially, it has both the citizens and geography in mind. It describes a particular group bearing a proper name and existing in a distinct land with cities and towns. The word for exalt is תְּרוֹמֵם־. In this instance, it's a positive expression. It means to be lifted into or exist in a position above all others.

What lifts a nation of cities filled with citizens intent on their homeland's welfare into this exalted status? It's just as Solomon wrote: righteousness. Christians know what he's talking about. Christ is our righteousness (1 Cor. 1:30). Through faith in God's Son, we stand before God blameless, holy, and capable of amending the sinful life so that we might serve faithfully in all things (2 Cor. 5:21; Matt. 5:13–16). Indeed, this faith produces deeds of righteousness (1 John 2:29; Eph. 2:4–10).

It is not a stretch to say one of faith's worthwhile fruits is mindful engagement for the sake of righteous government. And by righteous I don't mean Dominionism. I don't mean God expects Christians to take over, being the only ones capable of governance. I know some well-intentioned Christians in government who should be working at McDonald's instead. Besides, history has more than proven Dominionism to be a terrible idea.

Righteous government is good government. Good government holds to its divine ordination. It understands God extends His ruling authority to man, and the ones to whom He extends it are not occupying offices of self-serving privilege, nor are they to abuse their authority, becoming tyrannical overlords. Their task is to maintain good order according to God's natural and moral law. By doing this, they stem chaos, serve and protect citizens' lives and livelihoods, and maintain a context for the nation's overall wellbeing, care, and prosperity.

This is the optimal framework for a nation's welfare and the righteousness exalting it.

Now, ask yourself, "What can I do to strengthen our nation in this ordained purpose?" I assure you voting is not the only way. The preservation of a republic requires more than fleeting moments of patriotism or civic ritual. It demands a people who, by faith, understand engagement in the left-hand kingdom is a vocation as much as any other—ordained by God and governed by His moral law.

As citizens of this temporal kingdom and heirs of the eternal one, Christians are uniquely equipped to stand for righteousness, to serve with humility, and to resist tyranny in love. This is not a conflation of the kingdoms but a faithful walking within both: rendering unto Caesar what is Caesar's, while never ceasing to render unto God what is His. Only by maintaining this theological clarity can we serve both kingdoms well—and in doing so, be salt and light in a world desperate for both order and grace.

But theology, no matter how robust, is never enough on its own. The challenge we now face is not merely intellectual or civic. It is incarnational. The faithful Church must not only know what it believes about the public square but live that belief within it. Next, we'll explore what such incarnational courage looks like in practice, especially when the world is watching.

Chapter 12

Not Merely Theoretical but Incarnational

In the preface to his volume *The Great Divorce*, C. S. Lewis reminds wisely, "A sum can be put right: but only by going back till you find the error and working it afresh from that point, never by simply going on."[1] His point is well-taken. As the problem has now been extrapolated from multiple angles and in various degrees, things cannot continue as they are. The Church has too often treated public engagement as either optional or adversarial, when it is in fact a matter of faithfulness. Too many believers, trained in compartmentalized thinking, have chosen silence in the face of falsehood. If we are to move forward rightly, we must first recover the courage to speak the truth in love—publicly, humbly, and persistently.

For some, the urgent concern and subsequent call for Christian engagement in the public square are not apart from Christianity's persona as a truth-bearer. As was implied at the conclusion of the previous subsection titled "Lack of Conviction," to speak the truth is to demonstrate love.[2] Paul wrote, "through the church the manifold wisdom of God might now be made known" (Eph. 3:10). In other words, Paul names the church as truth's dispensary to the world.

Inversely, Owen Strachan comments, "This means, among other duties, exposing and confronting the false teaching."[3] Still, and as the Nietzschean adage says, sometimes the truth hurts.[4] But the pain it may cause is apart from lovelessness. While bringing stinging reprimand to the Galatians for embracing false theology leading to harmful practices, Paul asks rhetorically, "Have I then become your enemy by telling you the truth?" (Gal. 4:16). Of course, the answer must be no. Again, Strachan argues, "Paul and his peers had no choice between 'preach Christ' or 'deconstruct falsehood.' They had to do both."[5]

Indeed, by deconstructing falsehood, Paul proves himself a friend who loves the Galatian church. He is loving by not shrinking from delivering the truth. The apostle John echoes Paul, associating the demonstration of truth with the communication of genuine love: "Little children, let us not love in word or talk but in deed and in truth" (1 John 3:18).

Gaelan Gilbert might call such love a "dying to self—the death of self-love—for love of God and neighbor."[6] Natasha Crain calls for Christians to see what is happening in the world as an opportunity for mission.[7] Eric Metaxas shares Dietrich Bonhoeffer's call for love's demonstration in mission through action. He relays a portion from one of Bonhoeffer's addresses:

> If we want to be Christians, we must have some share in Christ's large-heartedness by acting with responsibility and in freedom when the hour of danger comes, and by showing a real sympathy that springs not from fear, but from the liberating and redeeming love of Christ for all who suffer. Mere waiting and looking on is not Christian behaviour. The Christian is called to sympathy and action, not in the first place by his own sufferings, but by the sufferings of his brethren, for whose sake Christ suffered.[8]

Understanding the public square as a social and political centrifuge, Erwin Lutzer has much to say concerning Christian love's demonstration. For him, disengagement from the public square is not an option for multiple reasons. First, he notes, "Politics cannot be separated from morality, and morality cannot be separated from Christianity."[9] He continues insisting anyone claiming allegiance to Christ cannot be quiet. Next, he caps the dramatic discussion by saying, "Let those who think it's okay to be indifferent about politics ask the Christians who lived under Nero or Nazi Germany."[10] This is to say genuine Christian love's vocalization and demonstration of truth affect entire societal constructs.

Regarding CRT, Lutzer considers ignoring its dangers unloving. He proposes CRT hurts the people it claims to help by demeaning minorities and perpetuating stereotypes.[11] On the other hand, Lutzer believes the Bible deals truthfully against it, confronting racism by emphasizing verities shared by all while simultaneously considering unique cultural distinctions.[12]

Therefore, in summary, equipped with God's Word, Christianity has the only real truth that can rightly engage in the public square ("go into the enemy territory")[13] in loving ways to rightly "distinguish between accepting a person and approving of their conduct."[14] Again, Lutzer understands love as truth's best vehicle, tenderly encouraging toward truth's expression wrapped in gentleness, respectful dialogue, and courtesy.

As Christians reach into the public square, sometimes to their demise, Eric Metaxas wonders hopefully if their kindly efforts will be what the listeners' deeper selves are longing to hear. Like Paul, he asks rhetorically, "Is it not possible that those whom we wish to evangelize are looking to us . . . to speak boldly on these things and fight for the truth?"[15] Mindful of natural law, Metaxas assumes objective truth's place within each human being, which includes a receptivity to love. When the truth is iterated, a part of the listener's self is eager for it to become dominant, knowing its dominance is necessary.

The further removed Christianity is from the public square, the more devastating the effects of its absence become. And so,

Michael Conway calls for the Church to "see itself in and with the world in which it finds itself,"[16] emphasizing the Church's natural place within culture. This is to say Christianity belongs in the public square.

Pondering Nietzsche's transvaluation of values, Carl Trueman suggests without the Church's direct influence, good eventually becomes evil, and that which was healthy becomes sick.[17] In his view, the sacred must inform the culture because "the abandonment of a sacred order leaves cultures without any foundation."[18] Richard John Neuhaus went so far as to refer to a public square absent Christianity as "the naked public square."[19]

Larry Golemon is only slightly concerned with the possible dangers of Christianity in the public square, reminding his reader that extreme piety imposed upon culture has resulted in long-lasting and unfortunate consequences. Apart from vivid examples like the Salem witch trials, which were acute manifestations of piety amok, Golemon points to more encompassing results, such as the 18th Amendment of the U.S. Constitution, inferring the tragic nationwide criminal enterprises born from Prohibition that remain today.[20]

Jo Renee Formicola is similarly mindful, highlighting the modern Roman Catholic Church's "approach to the role of religion in civil society" as little more than social activism leading to uncertainty.[21] President of the Davenant Institute and Senior Fellow of the Edmund Burke Foundation, W. Bradford Littlejohn, highlights Luther's Two Kingdoms doctrine as noticeably balancing. He acknowledges war's extreme prevalence leading up to the sixteenth century. However, following the Reformation, he concludes that war lost a significant measure of its Church-imbued sacredness, reducing its frequency. Littlejohn attributes this to the Two Kingdoms doctrine's associating war with temporal rule rather than spiritual.[22]

Pastoral Reflection: Prepared to Make a Defense

If love demands truth, and truth requires courage, then Christian engagement in the public square cannot be merely theoretical. It must become embodied—lived out in the faithful confessions and actions of those who carry Christ into the world. The theology of public witness is not abstract; it is incarnational. The Word becomes flesh again and again in the daily lives of believers who speak when silence is the easier path and stand when retreat would be safer. But what does this look like in practice? Sometimes, the boldest apologetics come not from pulpits or platforms but from the desks of ordinary classrooms. One such moment involved my daughter Evelyn. With that, I have a story to tell. It has two parts.

The story's first part occurred during my daughter Evelyn's science class. In short, her teacher asked the students to list ten "facts" about the Big Bang theory and the earth's formation. Evelyn did just that but only after first making something evident in the uppermost margin. At the top of her page, she wrote the words "Genesis 1" and "Jesus," both encased in hearts. (Of course she put hearts around those words. She's a girly girl. Girly girls put hearts on their page.) Right beside the hearted words, she wrote, "God created the heavens and the earth."

Next, she gave a title to her list. It read: "History and Earth Formation . . . Supposedly." Finally, she prefaced her list with the words, "Secularists believe that . . ." and then she provided ten examples. She would not say "facts" because the earth's formation as understood by the Big Bang is not factual but theoretical.

Before turning in the assignment, Evelyn sent me a screenshot of her page. I smiled and then commended her.

The second part of the story happened the next day. When I arrived home from the office, Evelyn came to find me and her mom in the kitchen. She wanted to tell us about a different scenario that happened in her history class the same day as the science class episode. Her teacher was introducing a segment on the Reformation. Along the way of his introduction, he explained it was doubtful Luther actually nailed his 95 Theses on the church door at Wittenberg. Unsurprisingly, Evelyn's ears perked, not because she believed him but because she was familiar with Lutheran history and knew better. She also picked up on what he was demonstrating, even though she couldn't necessarily articulate it.

It's relatively chic in education to reconstruct historical events—their contexts and characters. It's just as fashionable to apply biases relative to modern agendas. As a result, the "what" and "why" of what actually happened are often met with thick skepticism, even when immersed in source materials from first-hand witnesses providing detailed accounts.

Nevertheless, many in our schools have bought into this method. We're more than seeing it play out in the retelling of American history. Unfortunately, many of these historical critics are writing the next generation's textbooks. Nevertheless, this was not the point of Evelyn's story.

She told us her teacher insisted the Reformation really had nothing to do with issues of works-righteousness, implying most Christian denominations agree good works get people into heaven. Evelyn, being the forthright young girl she is, said audibly, "That's just not true." It was as if Paul's instruction in 2 Corinthians 10:5 was suddenly engaged in her heart, triggering her to "destroy arguments and every lofty opinion raised against the knowledge of God, and take every thought captive to obey Christ."

Indeed, if there was ever an argument or lofty opinion to destroy, it's the one muddying justification by grace through faith in Jesus Christ, the One who came to save us. As Luther so famously said, "If this article [justification] stands, the church stands; if it falls, the church falls."[23] In other words, if one's theology of justification is wrong, the person's salvation is in extreme jeopardy.

Now, to be fair, Evelyn likes this teacher very much. And he appears to like her too. He has nothing but wonderful things to say about her. He also claims Christianity, having told my daughter he attends a nearby non-denominational church. With these dynamics in place, a kindly exchange of ideas was possible, one allowing Evelyn, even if only for about twenty minutes, to assume a crucial role before a classroom of listening students, most of whom she knows are relatively unchurched or de-churched.

Doing my best to capture and summarize for you, it seems Evelyn's teacher insisted the God of the Bible grants favor leading toward heaven to those who are good. The way he explained it prompted Evelyn to conversely insist no one is good, not truly. She said all human beings are infected with the sin-nature; essentially we're all dead in our trespasses and sins. And because of this, not only are all our deeds—good or bad—horribly tainted with sin but we also can't do anything to save ourselves from this condition, let alone employ those deeds for personal rescue.

Her teacher's follow-up argument was it just didn't seem right that good deeds didn't play some sort of a role in the Christian tradition. At one point, referring directly to himself, he said if he gets into heaven, it would be, at least in part, because he was a pretty good guy.

Remaining within Christianity's genuine confines, Evelyn asked, "If good deeds get us into heaven, then what's the deal with Jesus?" She persisted, "He's kind of the center of everything Christians believe. If Christians can save themselves by doing good things, then why would Jesus even be necessary at all? That makes what He did kind of irrelevant." What she was trying to say is a Jesus who is only partly relevant for salvation is a Jesus who's completely irrelevant.

She went on to explain the whole reason Jesus came was to deal with and fix the sin problem, a predicament we were utterly powerless to change. He died on the cross and rose again to save everyone in the entire world from sin, death, and the consequence of hell. She also explained in remarkable detail that while good works do not play a part in our salvation, we should also be careful not to see them as apart from faith. They are fruits of faith. Christians—people who believe in Jesus as their Savior—do them not because they have to in order to get into heaven but because the Holy Spirit has worked faith in their hearts and now they want to do them.

Again, I'm summarizing the conversation. Still, those are the highlights. And those were a high school freshman's words to her history teacher . . . in a public school . . . offered without hesitation, and in front of her classmates.

I didn't ask her about any subsequent fallout from classmates, assuming some may have disapproved of her boldness. Frankly, I didn't feel the need to ask her and she didn't feel the need to mention it. For one, I'm continually amazed at how so many people know her name, and when she walks by, they go out of their way to say hello. I've seen it. It's heartwarming. My guess is her Christian frankness, rather than the typical attention-getting outspokenness from students drowning in gender confusion and pronouns and whatever else the culture is shoving down their throats, is probably a breath of fresh air to many around her. She certainly doesn't appear to be losing friends because of it, especially as she continues to articulate her faith so comfortably and splendidly.

Evelyn appears capable of seamlessly living Peter's encouragement to be "prepared to make a defense to anyone who asks you for a reason for the hope that is in you; yet do it with gentleness and respect" (1 Pet. 3:15). At a bare minimum, she's proof the rest of us can do the same, even in the proverbial belly of the beast.

Public education is by no means friendly to Christianity. In fact, I mentioned before how Evelyn appears relatively beloved by most who know her, both students and teachers. That said, there is one teacher she says hello to each morning who simply will not respond to her greeting.[24] If the teacher acknowledges her, it's with a glance before looking away. No reply. Nothing. Knowing the teacher, I think I understand why. Still, my wife and I encourage Evelyn to continue offering a friendly greeting, if only because a large part of demonstrating one's faith not only involves being immovably resolute concerning what's true and what isn't but also, as Peter noted, employing "gentleness and respect" as you do it.

Shoving the Christian faith down someone's throat doesn't work. But taking a stand when necessary—and doing so with a spirit of humility fixed on faithfulness to Christ—goes a long way, whether we realize it or not.

That said, and for as much as I'd like to brag about my daughter's courage, Peter's words weren't written to her alone. They were written to all of us. The Holy Spirit does not desire we shy away from opportunities to defend the faith, nor does He instill in us pompous motives intent on confrontation. Instead, He works a balance of boldness and grace, conviction and kindness. Like Evelyn, we can step into these moments—not to shout louder than the world, but to speak clearly and faithfully, confident the truth of Christ has the power to pierce the noise.

In the end, pushing back when pushing back is necessary isn't only about resisting falsehood. It's about offering something better: the truth of Jesus Christ and the hope against sin, death, and hell only He can provide.

Evelyn's witness is more than a proud parent's anecdote. It is a glimpse into the potential of every Christian—young or old—to confront error with conviction and extend truth with grace. Her example doesn't stand apart from the larger argument of this chapter but rather enfleshes it. The public square is not only filled with debates over policies or ideologies; it is also the hallway outside a history class, the silence of an unreplied greeting, or the choice to write "Genesis 1" at the top of a science assignment. These are the places where theology meets life and where the Christian must choose to live faithfully.

Indeed, the intersection between belief and action is neither passive nor privatized—but public, courageous, and alive. Evelyn's example, though seemingly modest, reminds us that engagement begins in the small arenas where truth is spoken and lived. But as history and Scripture repeatedly demonstrate, faithfulness in the small often prepares us for greater stages. What begins at a classroom desk may one day continue in a courtroom, a legislative chamber, or before a king. When Christians step into these spaces—armed not with arrogance but with the truth of Christ—they embody the same incarnational courage that has carried the Church through centuries.

I've been in situations where I've had to choose between integrity and ease. Years ago, a person I once considered a friend treated me in public as though we barely knew each other. I understood why. He was courting political donors who viewed my pro-life convictions as a liability. And so, in the presence of those influencers, he created conversational distance—adding layers to our relationship that made it appear thin or incidental. It was disappointing. Not simply because it revealed the fragility of our friendship, but because it showed how quickly convictions can be concealed when something is at stake.

Another time, I was standing in line at a fundraiser on Michigan's east side when a young woman behind me asked what I thought of the speaker on stage—a well-known politician.

"Do you really want to know?" I asked.

"Yes," she said, flatly. "Or I wouldn't have asked."

I answered honestly: "I'm not a fan. She tends to say just enough to get re-elected, and a lot of her policies are, frankly, reckless."

"She's my mom," she replied.

The bartender handed me my beer. I took it and said, "Well, like I said—some of your mom's policies are reckless." Then I walked back to my seat.

It was an awkward moment. But it didn't need additional commentary. Adding layers wouldn't have helped. We're often tempted to pad the truth—not to clarify but to protect ourselves. But when we do this, we lose more than we preserve. Ironically, it's the clean confession—the one that doesn't wobble or backpedal—that carries the most weight. When spoken plainly, truth may sting, but integrity remains intact.

This kind of plainspoken courage is the real measure of incarnational integrity—not eloquence, not polish, not cleverness. Just truth. Spoken aloud. Without layers. After all, not every believer will stand before a governor or a king, but every believer will be summoned into profound moments to bear witness.

❧

Chapter 13

Before Governors and Kings

Not every believer will stand in front of a classroom, let alone a king. But the call is the same. Whether in a hallway or a courtroom, whether in the presence of friends or governors, the Christian stands to bear witness. Christ prepared us for this moment long ago. He told His Christians rather plainly, "You will be dragged before governors and kings for my sake, to bear witness before them and the Gentiles" (Matt. 10:18). This is to say, the Two Kingdoms will meet, and as they do, Christians will necessarily respond. Acknowledging this concurrently, the Lord later prays for His people: "I do not ask that you take them out of the world, but that you keep them from the evil one. They are not of the world, just as I am not of the world. Sanctify them in the truth; your word is truth" (John 17:15–17).

Petitioning in this way, Jesus acknowledges the Two Kingdoms doctrine. Relative to this doctrine, He implies Christians will be sanctified carriers of divine truth into the kingdom of the left. This carrying will be according to the same source that establishes the kingdom of the right: the Word. Regardless the sphere, God's Word of truth, the Gospel, must prevail. The Gospel is God's gracious care for both.

Martin H. Scharlemann comments on Jesus's words in John 17, noting Christians exist in both kingdoms simultaneously, and as they do, they maneuver mindful that both kingdoms are in place to "serve [God's] larger purposes of grace."[1]

At this point, it should also be mentioned somewhat preemptively how far too many religious liberty resources muddy the subject of public square engagement by forcing unrelated biblical texts into predetermined ideologies. Galatians 5:13 is an oft-patriotically used example. It reads: "For you were called to freedom, brothers. Only do not use your freedom as an opportunity for the flesh, but through love serve one another." Unfortunately, handling the verse and its context with a sliver of honesty renders it unusable in religious liberty's first sphere of influence.

By "freedom" (ἐλευθερίᾳ),[2] it is easily determined that Paul indeed means Christian liberty but in the sense of freedom from the law's burden for salvation. R. C. H. Lenski notes the sentence's beginning (Ὑμεῖς),[3] arguing the apostle deliberately "places 'you' emphatically against the Judaizers,"[4] which is to say, those who were insisting the Galatian Christians bind themselves to former laws as necessary to salvation's equation. Therefore, this text is not applicable because Paul does not describe a Christian's duty relative to civil government.

Once again, apart from such examples, this project's thesis is not cloudy. It does not require eisegetical gymnastics. For the most part, the Lord's mandate that His Church engage with the world for the sake of the Gospel is its theological foundation. The Scriptures are laden with this universally accepted instruction. This mission-minded engagement is the primary thrust for persuading Christians to labor in the public square. Of course, to do so is to preserve religious liberty, which, as was partially extrapolated in the literature review above, maintains the Church's missiological heart: the freedom to preach and teach the Gospel for the extension of Christ's kingdom.[5]

Like all other missiological efforts in the Church, public square engagement is both centrifugal and centripetal in motion. It moves outward so that it might draw inward (Matt. 5:13–16;

24:14; 28:16–20; Mark 13:10; 16:15–16; Luke 24:46–49; John 20:19–23; Rom. 10:14–17; 1 Thess. 1:2–10; 1 Pet. 2:9–12; 3:15). As people are met, and the Gospel is given, hearts and minds are persuaded, and they join the believing community. Public square engagement not only participates in this divine arrangement but, more importantly, labors to preserve it, labeling it crucial to the Church's missiological identity.[6] Stepping forth from this essential premise, more appropriate texts come to mind, two of which may be sufficient for this project's case.

In 2 Corinthians, Paul establishes a two-part assertion when he writes: "For we must all appear before the judgment seat of Christ, so that each one may receive what is due for what he has done in the body, whether good or evil. Therefore, knowing the fear of the Lord, we persuade others. But what we are is known to God, and I hope it is known also to your conscience" (2 Cor. 5:10–11). First, Paul crisply notes Christians are accountable to God in all things, or as R. C. H. Lenski comments concerning both verses, "Our feeling toward the Lord controls all that we do in regard to men."[7]

Phillip Edgcumbe Hughes explains further, acknowledging Paul "has a deep consciousness of the awe which should be inspired in the heart of every servant who will be required to give an account of his stewardship to his master."[8] Lenski and Hughes understand whatever a Christian does or does not do as he meets with the world must align with God's will.

According to this will, Paul encourages a specific behavior born from the previously mentioned accountability: deliberate dialogue fashioned to persuade (πείθομεν).[9] Receptive to the word's durative sense, Lenski interprets it to mean "we are busy persuading," which is to say, such dialogue is an ongoing and regular activity for Christians as they interact with one another and the surrounding world.[10] It is no surprise, then, that Lenski would also admit persuasive dialogue "is still the great task of the gospel ministry."[11]

Having cemented a relatively simple proposition, Paul employs a unique blend of theological and diplomatic terms further along in the same chapter. He writes later in chapter 5: "Therefore, we are ambassadors for Christ, God making his appeal through us" (2 Cor. 5:20). To use the phrase "we are ambassadors of God" (πρεσβεύομεν ὡς τοῦ θεοῦ) is for Paul to paint a unique image, one portraying official dignitaries living in a foreign land and pressing for the interests of their homeland and its ruler. Indeed, this speaks to Paul's point. Christians represent God's interests in the mortal sphere.

Hughes agrees, noting that Paul means for his reader to recall an "ambassador acts and speaks not only on behalf of but also in the place of the sovereign from whom he has received his commission. It is his duty to proclaim faithfully and precisely the message entrusted to him by the sovereign."[12]

David E. Garland addresses the natural flavor of Paul's words, reminding readers, "Surviving documents and inscriptions that provide us with some record of ancient diplomacy make it quite clear that envoys were usually sent to others as a sign of friendship and goodwill, to establish a relationship, to renew friendly relations, or to make an alliance."[13] Garland's point caps one of this project's noted assumptions, which is engagement in the public square for the preservation of religious liberty is good, namely, beneficial for all involved.

Admittedly, the previously mentioned texts do not speak directly to public square engagement. Few texts do. They merely determine an arena for its legitimacy already understood by the Church's missiology. Beyond this, its enactment is just as available to the Bible's reader throughout the Old and New Testaments. However, Paul's necessary demonstrations in the book of Acts seem most appropriate. Nevertheless, before visiting with Paul's circumstances, the usual suspects of Matthew 22:15–22 and Romans 13:1–7 should at least be considered, even if only briefly.

Concerning Matthew 22, two warring factions confront the Lord: the Pharisees and the Herodians. In verse 17, the Pharisees ask Jesus, "Is it lawful to pay taxes to Caesar, or not?" The question is a trap designed to enable charges from either of the enjoining parties. The Pharisees' words are meant to force Jesus to take a public stand on a volatile issue.[14] Contextually, the Pharisees despised Caesar and believed paying him taxes was to disavow God. The Herodians were devout supporters of King Herod Antipas and, as such, were willing subscribers to Caesar's rule.

For Jesus to side with one party would be to alienate the other. Nevertheless, the Lord proves by His answer His divine brilliance, electing instead to define what C. L. Blomberg noted as "the Reformation doctrine of differing spheres of authority for government and religion and proved foundational for the American constitutional separation of church and state."[15] Blomberg means what has already been established: the Two Kingdoms doctrine.

For Christ to say in verse 21, "Therefore render to Caesar the things that are Caesar's, and to God the things that are God's" (Matt. 22:21), the Two Kingdoms are divinely admitted. Conversely, for the church to deny its duty to the state is to fracture the doctrine. Likewise, for the state to demand its citizens to worship Caesar as a god fractured it too.[16] Succinctly, the kingdom of the right hand owns worship, while the kingdom of the left hand owns civic duty. However, as will be shown from Paul's words in Romans 13, both reside beneath God's supreme rule and must bend to His will.

Concerning Romans 13:1–7, it is generally accepted within conservative Christianity that the mandate given is done so prescriptively, not descriptively.[17] In other words, Paul is describing what Christians owe a government that holds to its divine ordination. Having called the civil rulers "God's servant for your good" (13:4), the following text in verses 8 through 10 must necessarily affirm any law acting contrary to the law of love and ultimately leading to harm is beyond the government's scope.

Accordingly, theologian and philosopher Francis A. Schaeffer insists:

> The civil government, as all of life, stands under the law of God. In this fallen world God has given us certain offices to protect us from the chaos which is the natural result of that fallenness. But when any office commands what is contrary to the Word of God, those who hold that office abrogate their authority and they are not to be obeyed and that includes the state.[18]

For Schaeffer, an ungodly government required a Christian's disobedience, similar to that which Peter and the apostles demonstrated in Acts 5:29. Even more so, for governing authorities to hinder the Gospel, that is, to suppress religious liberty, would be to engage in the citizenry's cruelest harm, thereby requiring the apostles to disobey men in order to remain faithful to God. Like Schaeffer, C. K. Barrett joins a Christian's respect for the civil government only to the nature of its ordination, noting honor is due "not because they are powerful and influential men, but because they have been appointed by God."[19]

As was previously mentioned, the Scriptures are well-supplied with relative examples concerning believers engaging in the public square, whether for or in opposition to the established rulers.[20] Among these, 1 Timothy 2:1–6 has already been mentioned. It should be noted in this text, Paul employs a unique word potentially adding dimension to a Christian's civic concerns.

In the text's first verse, Paul teaches Christians to offer "supplications, prayers, intercessions, and thanksgivings" (1 Tim. 2:1) concerning the state and its citizens. Interestingly, amid the steady cadence of recognizable terms, Paul employs ἐντεύξεις (intercessions) often synonymously with intervention. However, James Strong further interprets ἐντεύξεις to mean appeal through formal conversation or interview.[21] In other words, to intercede requires reciprocating dialogue.

The *Theological Dictionary of the New Testament* notes a similar usage throughout history. For example, ἐντεύξεις is used in Plato's *Politicus* to describe general dealings, and in particular, negotiations with pirates. Aristotle's *Rhetorica* employs it to mean interpersonal dialogue. Flavius Josephus uses it in his *Antiquitates* to describe the claims of Queen Cleopatra VII Philopator to Judaea,[22] likely including Cleopatra's intercessions with Antony concerning Herod the Great.[23]

While speculative, it certainly seems possible that by using ἐντεύξεις, Paul does not mean for all Christians to expect back-and-forth conversations with God. Few in history (Paul being one) were elected for such experiences. Instead, a Christian's civic concern rises vertically through supplication and prayer while also engaging horizontally relative to the ones in earthly authority. This is to say that Christians plead with God in the kingdom of the right hand while not neglecting their civic duty to plead also with authorities in the kingdom of the left.

Logically, a prescriptive thanksgiving concludes Paul's catechesis, revealing his hopeful outcome: Christians would do this and, subsequently, enjoy peacefully led, godly, and dignified lives free to share the Gospel (1 Tim. 2:2–4). Insinuation or not, Paul embodied this dual-directional activity throughout his ministry. A tour through the book of Acts reveals this.

The tour arrives first at Acts 16:16–40, where Paul is arrested, beaten, and jailed by town magistrates for exorcising a demon-possessed slave girl whose fortune-telling abilities were profitable for her owners. The following day, the magistrates gave orders to release Paul (and Silas, who was with him). However, Paul invoked his rights as a Roman citizen, reminding the officers he was beaten and jailed without a trial, eventually making a demand of his offenders that was awarded in course.[24] Paul's demand was an unquestioned claim requiring the magistrates to escort him to the city gates, thereby serving punishment through embarrassment to the unjust rulers before the entire community.

Paul behaves similarly in Acts 22:22–29. Having once again been unjustly arrested, before the commander could have him flogged, Paul invoked his rights, asking rhetorically, "Is it lawful for you to flog a man who is a Roman citizen and uncondemned?" (Acts 22:25). Fearful of his disregard for Paul's right to a fair trial, the commander released him. However, Paul remained under his jurisdiction, which Paul freely obeyed, even though it extended Paul's troubles, eventually leading him to stand before Governor Felix.

Having already established his case in Acts 22:6–10 as religious discrimination, Paul established the same premise before Felix in Acts 24:14–21. Imprisoned but not executed, Paul stayed the course for two more years, pleading similarly before King Herod Agrippa and Governor Festus.

To summarize, even as Paul was no stranger to pursuing legal means, his efforts served the goal he enunciated in 1 Timothy 2:1–6 and hoped for in Romans 13:1–7. Simply put, Christians labor in the public square because, first, they know God desires all to be saved. Second, by holding the government to its divine mandate and by maintaining religious liberty, a peaceful and quiet life lived in all godliness is a citizen's sunlit upland of possibility. Third, religious liberty allows for the extension of the kingdom through the free preaching and teaching of the Gospel, which Paul heralds as the "power of God unto salvation" (Rom. 1:16).

In conclusion, it is worth acknowledging doctrine never lives in a vacuum. The Scriptures surveyed thus far are not abstract blueprints for theoretical engagement; they are meant to be enacted. They speak to real Christians, in real places, facing real challenges in a fallen world. The call to determined participation in the public square—rooted in biblical precedent—is not just about preserving religious liberty as a concept but about stewarding the gift of the Gospel in time and space.

To that end, the principles become most vivid when they move from page to pavement, from the pulpit to the personal, where the Gospel-shaped conscience is summoned to act and persistence is tested. Consider the following snow-covered sidewalks of real life.

Pastoral Reflection: Persistence and Determination

I do not like snow. Still, I do my best to muscle through winter's frigid dreariness here in Michigan, finding a sliver of comfort in words like those of the Spanish adage, "Little by little, one travels far." For me, this is to say each day is a moment closer to summer, or as I've said to my children on occasion during winter, attempting to be positive and yet confusing them, "No matter the weather, there's more 'summer' in today than there was yesterday. Even better, there's less 'summer' in today than there will be in tomorrow."

There is the oft-quoted saying attributed to Calvin Coolidge, which I also happen to have taped to the bookshelf beside me:

> Nothing in this world can take the place of persistence. Talent will not; nothing is more common than unsuccessful men with talent. Genius will not; unrewarded genius is almost a proverb. Education will not; the world is full of educated derelicts. Persistence and determination alone are omnipotent.[25]

I appreciate that quotation. It defines my disgust for the word "can't." When you say something can't be done, you can expect me to be the first in line to push back with ideas on how it can. My doctoral program allowed seven years for completion. The moment I was accepted into it, I didn't have seven years to spare, so I committed to accomplishing it no more than three. Knowing my life's pace, someone close to me insisted it was an unrealistic goal, inferring, "It can't be done." That's all the challenge I needed, and therefore, I did it. Yes, it was ungodly difficult. But it wasn't impossible, if only because there was no "can't" in my mathematics.

Far beyond all these things, there remains an unalterable difference between being undeterred and being foolish. *Touchstone* magazine once quoted me as saying, "The value of any particular belief or effort cannot necessarily be judged by the amount of courage it takes to defend it. Foolishness can very easily be mistaken for courage."[26] Concerning what I've written so far, there's a "can't" or two that one should never approach with a confident, "Oh yes, I can!" To do so would be to demonstrate a foolish kind of determination.

I can't rescue myself from sin. I can't earn my eternal life. In that sense, Coolidge's quote has a flaw. Of course, I understand Coolidge's emphasis. Nevertheless, persistence and determination are by no means all-powerful, and as such, thankfully, they do not figure into God's salvific calculus. If they did, we'd be lost. Only Christ's persistence will do. Only Christ's determination can establish our eternal future.

Relative to the things of God, does that mean persistence and determination mean nothing? Not at all. The Bible definitely encourages believers to pursue and exhibit these characteristics. But it does so after faith, not before. Only by the power of the Holy Spirit can a Christian be found undeterred in this life. Again, this divine obstinance is not given so we somehow start thinking we participate in or earn our place before God. Christ already earned that place by His life, death, and resurrection. He gives it to us. Faith receives it. From there, the conscious aspect of this becomes a deliberate desire to be undeterred in faithfulness to the gift-giver, Jesus.

It's from there the writer to the Hebrews encourages his fellow Christians to "run with endurance the race that is set before us, looking to Jesus, the founder and perfecter of our faith" (Heb. 12:2). It's with that truth in hand that Paul so confidently announces, "Be steadfast, immovable, always abounding in the work of the Lord, knowing that in the Lord your labor is not in vain" (1 Cor. 15:58).

It's with that foundational understanding that Paul not only warns, "Therefore let anyone who thinks that he stands take heed lest he fall" (1 Cor. 10:12) while James determines with incredible assurance, "Blessed is the man who remains steadfast under trial, for when he has stood the test he will receive the crown of life, which God has promised to those who love him" (James 1:12).

Yes, winters pass. The snow melts. The natural world suddenly becomes just one more reminder of persistence's glorious import. The seemingly dead trees break forth with springtime sprouts, foretelling summer's determination to arrive—and it does so undeterred. That's the truth.

Similarly, some Christians press forward into the public square with persistence and determination, intent on embracing the biblical mandate to engage, while others double down on the idea that Christians should stay in their lanes and let things be as they will. Determination and persistence are displayed in both circumstances. However, the value of genuine fortitude only comes when it's anchored in truth.

For Christians, we have Christ, and so we can be determined alongside Paul and say, "For I decided to know nothing among you except Jesus Christ and him crucified" (1 Cor. 2:2). That kind of determination, much to the world's astonishment, forms the very guts of the Christian faith. In other words, the most steadfast earthly pursuits all pale in comparison to the endurance capability of faith.

This faith extends into the realm of government, acknowledging governments rise and fall. Leaders come and go. Christ remains. His persistence is our salvation. His endurance is our victory. In that, we find the truest definition of determination is to take a firm aim at the only truly lasting thing.

And that's the very ground upon which the Church stands when she steps into the public square.

Engaging with the world for the sake of Christ is not done in the hope that temporal governments will last forever or liberty will be unending. Rather, it is done because the Church, standing as ambassador and intercessor, is tethered to something eternal. The courage to step forward comes not from a misplaced confidence in human strength but from a fixed certainty Christ has gone before us—and remains with us still.

The examples surveyed in the previous portion—the apostle Paul in Acts, Jesus before the Pharisees and Herodians, the exhortations in Romans and Timothy—converge to display a single truth: Christians are called not to be silent witnesses to the world's decay but to be determined and persistent participants in the preservation of space for the Gospel's proclamation. The biblical record is not bashful about this. It shows believers appealing to governors, standing before kings, enduring public scorn, and enduring in truth. And it shows them doing so with a clear conscience and a clear purpose.

Ultimately, the Church's participation in the public square is not about imposition. It is certainly not about nationalism or nostalgia. It is about love—love for the God who gave His Son for the world, and love for the neighbor. Engaging in this love is risky. Sacred determination always is. After all, we've been told plainly that as we are faithful in this way, we may find ourselves standing before governors and kings to bear witness. Matthew 10:18, much like Romans 13:1–7, is not merely descriptive. It is prescriptive. And it is a promise bearing the Lord's blessing.

As believers carry His blessing into the public square incarnationally, they do so within systems shaped by legal precedent, philosophical worldview, and cultural memory. The theological call to bear witness intersects with the frameworks either accommodating or resisting that witness.

And so, the question arises: What kind of system have we inherited in America? Is it one that forbids the Church's public voice or one that protects and even welcomes it? This next chapter considers that question by examining the history and meaning behind the oft-invoked phrase "the separation of Church and State."

❧

Chapter 14

SEPARATION OR ACCOMMODATION?

Before we can faithfully navigate our public witness, we must understand the legal and cultural terrain underfoot. The phrase "the separation of Church and State"—though often misused or misunderstood—has shaped how religious liberty is applied and perceived in America. What follows is not only a historical scan but a theological evaluation of the two dominant schools of interpretation governing the Church's place in civic life: separationism and accommodationism.

Visiting history, John Witte Jr. reveals the "church and state" phrase's traceability to first-century Christianity, eventually being "captured in the Christian clergy's perennial call of subsequent centuries for 'freedom of the church'—or what the Edict of Milan of 313 had called the 'free exercise and practice of religious groups.'"[1] He continues by describing five deliberate reasons behind the Founders' employment of the ideology in early America.

1. "To protect church affairs from state intrusion, the clergy from the magistracy, church properties from state interference, ecclesiastical rules and rites from political coercion and control."[2]

2. To protect the state from the church, noting that much abuse has come among societies where religion and government have been wholly united.[3]
3. To defend individual liberty against intrusion from the church or state or their collaboration.[4]
4. To protect "individual states from interference by the federal government in governing local religious affairs."[5]
5. "To protect society and its members from unwelcome participation in and support for religion."[6]

None of the previously mentioned premises establish absolute separation. Witte says as much throughout his article, noting it was not until "the turn of the nineteenth century, the language of separation of church and state also began to fuel broader campaigns to remove traditional forms and forums of religion in law, politics, and society altogether."[7] He first points to the less-than-congenial debates between Thomas Jefferson's Republican party and John Adams's Federalist party. In short, each attacked the other's political positions theologically—one calling the other the anti-Christ and the other retorting likewise.

Witte describes the ever-increasing blast radius that resulted as "the opening shots in a century-long American battle over the meaning and means of separating church and state," adding that the conflict's campaign was "fought in Congress and in the courts, in states and on the frontier, in churches and in the schools, in clubs and at the ballot box."[8]

The 1947 Supreme Court decision in *Everson v. Board of Education* would dramatically cap a centuries-long battle. It was there "the Court applied the First Amendment Establishment Clause to the states: 'Congress shall make no law . . .', now became, in effect, 'Governments of any kind shall make no law respecting an establishment of religion'—a rejection of the original federalist understanding of church and state."[9] Witte adds that Justice Hugo Black, a central figure for pure separationism, heavy-handedly applied a strict separationist view to the Establishment Clause, an ideology he learned as a member of the Ku Klux Klan.

Black's legacy appears to be apart from America's history, which was an intentional attempt to "strike a balance between coercion and freedom."[10] Professor of American Intellectual and Cultural History at Georgia State University, David Sehat, would call such a balance utopian, arguing that without strict separation, the truest goals of a democratic government set toward equality is all but disemboweled.[11]

Others believe as Sehat, some going so far as to forbid the influence of religious conscience in the public square entirely. Former European Court of Human Rights judge András Sajó is one, insisting that for as stabilizing as religion might be, America's current form of government, constitutionalism, does not permit religious influence, and the only reason it continues to occur is because of government benevolence. Sajó continues, "The logic of contemporary liberalism compels the state, even in constitutionally secular countries such as France or Turkey, to adopt a positive, benevolent attitude toward religions, mostly for good reasons. Such attitudes flow not only from the political necessity of respecting powerful groups but from the obligations of tolerance."[12]

For Sajó, a constitutional framework is purposely designed to prevent religious infiltration and influence. It is purely and fundamentally secular. Although, secularism "as a social fact and as a feature of constitutionalism, is vulnerable to the challenges of strong religion because of its uncertainty as a legal concept,"[13] which is to say secularism operates "at a social or cultural level," making it susceptible to religious influence.

For those pursuing the so-called balance intended by the Founders, this becomes the regular in-road for continued pressure from religious groups. Sajó believes "'secularism' . . . as an accepted concept having constitutional value"[14] will inevitably be weakened by religion's participation in the public square, becoming "subject to the unprincipled wishy-washiness of balancing—or disregarded in the name of proportionality—for the sake of free exercise of religion."[15]

The alternate view, accommodationism, sees the relationship between Church and State far differently. In short, accommodationism "rests on the belief that government and religion are compatible and necessary to a well-ordered society."[16] It further contends the First Amendment cultivates Church and State cooperation rather than disinterest or enmity. Therefore, it allows the government to promote religion but it does not allow the official establishment of religious institutions.

It was Abraham Kuyper, the late nineteenth-century Reformed pastor and prime minister of the Netherlands, who so famously said, "here is not one square inch in the whole domain of our human existence over which Christ, who is sovereign, does not cry 'Mine!'"[17] But that is not all he said. He prefaced his words by insisting no part of humanity's mental frame can be wholly divided from its other parts. By this, he intended to show Christ's role as ruler over both spheres, commonly referred to in theology as the Two Kingdoms doctrine.

Perhaps more interesting are the words sent by James Madison, the fourth president of the United States, to Frederick Schaeffer in New York in December of 1821. Schaeffer, a Lutheran pastor (and, as such, an inheritor of Luther's world-shaping examination of the relationship between Church and State), presided over the cornerstone ceremony for St. Matthew Lutheran Church in New York City. Doing so, he wrote and preached a sermon in which Luther's Two Kingdoms theology was crisply spoken.[18] Schaeffer sent the sermon to Madison, who later replied:

> It is a pleasing and persuasive example of pious zeal, united with pure benevolence and of a cordial

> attachment to a particular creed, untinctured with sectarian illiberality. It illustrates the excellence of a system which, by a due distinction, to which the genius and courage of Luther led the way, between what is due to Caesar and what is due God, best promotes the discharge of both obligations. The experience of the United States is a happy disproof of the error so long rooted in the unenlightened minds of well-meaning Christians, as well as in the corrupt hearts of persecuting usurpers, that without a legal incorporation of religious and civil polity, neither could be supported. A mutual independence is found most friendly to practical Religion, to social harmony, and to political prosperity.[19]

Madison describes the doctrine as best iterating what is due to God and what is owed to Caesar. As with Luther, who forbade Christians from trying to establish "the authority of worldly legal order,"[20] Madison denounces with capable eloquence dominionistic doctrines as well-meaning but false. He does the same with those who press for absolute separation of Church and State. In other words, for Madison, one of the nation's founders, drafters of its constitution, and first presidents, the Two Kingdoms doctrine delineates the best meaning of the phrase "the separation of Church and State." Additionally, the doctrine has the best grip on how and where the separation begins and ends.

To close, the doctrinal boundaries between separationism and accommodationism are more than matters of historical interpretation or jurisprudential theory. They manifest in practical ways, especially when the Church is confronted with real-time cultural and political pressures. The abstract principles of religious liberty inevitably descend into the concrete decisions of individual believers and pastors alike—especially when confronted by competing allegiances to conscience, confession, and the public good. The following account provides a modern instance where such tensions rise to the surface and reveal the fragility—or the fortitude—of one's theological commitments in action.

Of course, these doctrines are not left in the halls of theology. They show themselves, either well-formed or tragically malnourished, in the pulpits and voting booths of the present age. The following episode reveals what happens when theological compromise masquerades as pastoral care.

Pastoral Reflection: Unity at All Costs?

Sipping the last of a forty-five-year-old scotch while watching *Beetlejuice* with my wife at 10:00 p.m. on the eve of a rather significant speech, I leaned toward my movie partner and said, "I still have no idea what I'm going to say at tomorrow's conference." Of course, there I was using my time wisely. But she didn't point out the obvious. Instead, she comforted me with her usual poise. She reminded me inspiration is easy enough to find, and being such a wordy guy, filling up forty-five minutes of space has never been a problem for me.

She was right on both accounts. And so later that night, to find my inspiration, I went where everyone goes: social media, in particular, Facebook. I went to see what the experts on everything were saying about everything. Within seconds, I could barely contain my desire to start writing because I landed on a post from a fellow Lutheran pastor who, with a presidential election on the very near horizon, offered unsolicited counsel to Christians about voting. He wrote the following:

"In Christian liberty, vote for whichever imperfect candidate you like, as your conscience guides you, and don't let anybody give you a guilt trip about it. Live in the freedom of grace!"[21]

Now, to summarize his inherent point.

"God doesn't care which candidate you choose in the upcoming election, as long as you mean well by your choice. And if anyone begrudges your choice, let them be damned."

There were already eighty-two comments beneath the post when I first landed on it. Scrolling through, I could see a majority were in support. Fifty-eight people "liked" it, fourteen of whom were Lutheran pastors, each having hundreds of parishioners within their spiritual care. Some of these pastors wrote things like: "Good to be reminded God is in control." Another encouraged people not to bother voting at all, writing, "Voting is the illusion of choice, imho. I'd rather sort my sock drawer. Lol."

Still, another pastor unpacked the original post, sharing more thoroughly what he actually teaches the people in his care. He wrote, essentially—assuming they were Christians—as long as his people believed in their hearts what they were doing with their votes was right, that is, they had the best interest of their fellow citizens and nation in mind, they were free to choose any candidate they liked and be comfortably free from the fear of offending God. He ended his summary with a comment about Christians who choose political candidates who actively pursue the murder of the unborn, confuse natural law, and openly persecute the Christian Church:

"I cannot condemn Democrat voters as unchristian or unbelieving if they sincerely think that more evil and harm is being done by those for whom I would vote. Similarly, I would hope they would not so judge me or my friendship."

Imagine that phrase being spoken by a German pastor in 1934. Imagine a pastor saying to his Christian parish, "I cannot condemn the National Socialist Party (the Nazi party) voters as unchristian or unbelieving if they sincerely think that more actual evil and harm is being done to our world by those for whom I would vote."

The truth is, you don't have to imagine it. It was said. It was spoken by many German Lutheran pastors in the early 1930s as the Nazis were coming to power.[22] These pastors—ill-tuned to the coming devastation and less concerned for saying hard things lest they offend their congregations—encouraged their people to simply go about their business, to not forfeit peace between Christians by being judgmental of one another's party affiliations, knowing in the end, it probably didn't matter anyway because God was in control and would certainly ordain the outcome.[23]

The primary concern was to ensure the twenty-eight regional church bodies in Germany remained united for the country during a post–World War I time of national distress.[24] Drawing on the words of my fellow clergyman from today, I can compare them to those of Rev. Emanuel Hirsch, a leading liberal theologian of the time, whose similar preaching and teaching eventually proved quite useful to the Nazi Party.[25]

Contextually, during the 1930s and up until the end of the war in 1945, the Christian church in Germany was divided. This struggle is known as the *Kirchenkampf* (church struggle), which essentially pitted all the Lutheran churches in the country against two theological camps.[26] On one side of the conflict were the *Deutsche Christen* (German Christians), primarily comprising the more contemporary, liberal-leaning, and culturally friendly churches. Hirsch was a leader in this group.[27]

On the other side you had the not-so-mushy *Bekennende Kirche* (Confessing Church), which was comprised of the more confessional, conservative churches—the ones who held to the Scriptures as the sole source for faith, life, and practice, to confessional documents as true expositions of the Word of God, to the biblical doctrines as objective, immutable truth, and the standard for right and wrong. Dietrich Bonhoeffer emerged from this theological camp.[28]

Hirsch was intent on bringing the two groups together in nonjudgmental peace, and his efforts began by teaching what you heard one of my fellow Lutheran pastors say already—theologically speaking, voting is the illusion of choice and it is wrong to say any party is more favorable to God than another.[29] Interestingly, if you compare Hirsch's early writings to the ones he wrote once Hitler was in power, you'll notice in the beginning, he preached the churchy, bubbly mush of "unity, no doctrinal divides, no matter what!"

But then, in the thick of Nazi power, his most notable work, *Deutschlands Schicksal*, aimed directly at the Confessing Church's opposition to the Nazis. He insisted they stood apart from God's will by promoting division. He wrote harshly about them and pompously of himself, "the only point of unity in Germany, for the more noble among us is the concern for Germany's fate."[30] Another interesting fact that shouldn't surprise you: While writing this volume, Hirsch was also working on a side project of rewriting three of the four Gospels to remove their more Jewish elements.[31]

Of course, what was happening in the churches was known to Hitler. In fact, it was through the liberal churches that Hitler worked to impose what was known as the *Gleichschaltung* doctrine (bringing into line). He aimed at these free-wheeling churches primarily because they were malleable, already being so friendly with the culture and having shown themselves to have little ability to discern, and even less fortitude for resistance.[32] They were less inclined to say a Christian was obligated to vote a certain way, leaning instead toward ecumenism—unity at all costs.

Hitler elected to use the voices in these churches because when it came to their Christian viscera, he considered them, in his own words, "flabby."[33] And he was right. These churches would very quickly be found embracing and defending the Nazi

Party. They became convinced National Socialism would, by God's divine hand, bring nothing but good to the world through what they became convinced were most important: Hitler's social and racial agendas.[34]

Now, consider again my fellow Lutheran pastor's concerning words regarding the party behind all these efforts and the voters who will usher them in:

"I cannot condemn Democrat voters as unchristian or unbelieving if they sincerely think that more evil and harm is being done by those for whom I would vote."

He wrote these words at a time when killing a full-term baby in the womb was legal. He tapped these words even as the confusion of natural law became normalized.

This episode serves as more than a lamentation of pastoral compromise. It is a direct illustration of what happens when separationism is taken to its extreme and accommodationism is stripped of its doctrinal anchor. When Christians forsake theological clarity for cultural comfort—claiming neutrality in moments of moral crisis—they do not preserve peace; they facilitate surrender. The Two Kingdoms doctrine, rightly understood, neither silences the Church nor baptizes the state. Instead, it calls for a faithful engagement that discerns where Caesar's realm ends and God's truth must speak. In the face of rising secularism and the ever-blurring boundaries of cultural orthodoxy, such discernment is not optional. It is essential.

Section 3

Chapter 15

Loose Nails and Last Stands

American Christians face a narrowing corridor of political engagement. As the moral foundations of public life erode, the question is no longer which party reflects Christian values perfectly, but whether any remain close enough to permit faithful participation.

While no political party can claim perfection, the Republican Party remains, at present, the only major political institution in the United States whose candidates and initiatives come anywhere close to reflecting God's will for civil government. It is the only party in today's American system that still grants orthodox Christianity a meaningful voice.[1] The Democrat Party, in contrast, does not do this. Its aims, rhetoric, and platform stand entirely counter to Christianity.[2]

One might wonder about the Libertarians. Pure Libertarianism often claims to provide space for Christianity, but in truth, its foundational plank—absolute individual freedom in all things—proves to be little more than radical individualism cake with liberty-flavored frosting.[3] When lived out, this philosophy tends to lead not toward order and flourishing but rather toward cities ravaged by drugs, graves filled with unborn children, and clinics where euthanasia is celebrated as autonomy. Ultimately, it offers nothing but the false promise of freedom without form.

By contrast, the Republican Party has long stood as the more compatible choice for Christians, not in every respect, of course, but certainly in ways concerning morality and natural law, resting closest to the Christian conscience.[4] And yet a critical question arises: How long will this compatibility last?

Regrettably, the answer appears bleak: probably not for much longer.

The principle is not complicated. Even the smallest details matter. A teaspoon and a tablespoon may seem like minor variations, but in baking, a recipe calling for three teaspoons of salt ruined by mistakenly using three tablespoons delivers an entirely different, likely inedible, result. Similarly, a person deviating by a single degree on a journey may find over time, the deviation leads to a far different destination than intended.

George Herbert captured this well: "For want of a nail the shoe is lost, for want of a shoe the horse is lost, for want of a horse, the rider is lost."[5] In other words, small deviations can have catastrophic consequences. The rider checks his horse's shoes not out of paranoia but because he knows a missing nail can cascade into disaster.

In politics, as in most sciences, small deviations at the root can yield massive distortions downstream. One of the clearest contemporary examples of this principle is the 2015 *Obergefell v. Hodges Supreme Court* decision, which affirmed the right to same-sex marriage. At the time, it was presented as a minor deviation—merely an expansion of marital rights. But less than a decade later, the compounding effects are unmistakable. In 2024, we find ourselves in a cultural moment where people are not only marrying pets, computers, and robots, but where traditional beliefs about marriage are increasingly criminalized.[6] We're also witnessing demands for public endorsement of gender ideologies so unmoored from reality that they produce mass confusion.[7]

That single lost nail in 2015 has altered the direction of society in world-shaping ways.

Of course, the Democratic Party was already lost in this regard. It has long been the party of abortion. Its earlier rhetoric—"safe but rare"—at least feigned moral hesitance. That pretense has disappeared. In 2022, for example, Michigan amended its constitution to permit abortion at every stage of pregnancy.[8] Within the party's platform, abortion is not merely defended—it is promoted as healthcare, even exalted as a sacrament of bodily autonomy. Adoption is denigrated. And among party faithful, a woman is a "champion" for having an abortion, a "goddess" if she's had several.

Given this trajectory, what are Christians to make of recent shifts in the Republican Party? The 2024 platform officially opened the door to abortion acceptability. It removed the clear, longstanding language advocating for the complete abolition of abortion and instead emphasized a 14th Amendment "leave-it-to-the-states" approach. The reasoning was political: after the 2020 election, President Trump concluded an explicitly pro-life stance would only be a burden to the party, costing future electoral victories.[9] And while I fully supported all three of Donald Trump's presidential bids, he couldn't be more wrong in this regard.

For one, numerous statistics indicate a growing pro-life sentiment among younger Americans, which is a demographic the Republican Party is desperate to claim.[10] If that trend continues, will the Republican Party's platform undermine it? What will happen now that another nail has been lost from the shoe?

There is another concern of equal magnitude: the Republican Party's quiet abandonment of its opposition to same-sex marriage. The platform language affirming marriage as the union of one man and one woman was included in both the 2016 and 2020 versions. But in 2024, it was removed entirely. Another nail—gone.

Not coincidentally, the Republican National Committee and its affiliates are now partnering with the Log Cabin Republicans, the largest conservative LGBTQ group in the United States.[11] Their leader, Charles Moran, openly celebrated the change. In his view, the platform's revision is not the end but the beginning, signaling, in his words, "bigger and better things" for the gay and transgender community's participation in Republican politics.[12] In a recent interview, he proudly noted the party's "180-degree flip" between 2004 and 2024. However, his confidence turned to concern when asked about current state-level efforts by conservatives to pass anti-transgender legislation. Moran responded that the Log Cabin Republicans have no intention of excluding transgender ideology from their coalition. In other words, continued pressure to reshape the Republican platform should be expected.

Again, to what destination are we heading? Where will the Republican rider and his horse arrive in four, eight, or twelve years? Are we approaching a point where the rider can marry his horse, who now identifies as a cow, and both campaign for bovine pronouns to be federally recognized?

I hope I'm wrong. But I worry these increasingly loose shoes may carry the Republican Party, the last remaining home for Christians in American politics, to distant shores where Christians can no longer go. Not merely because we're unwanted, but because our conscience, shaped by God's Word, forbids us to follow.

For Christians trying to walk this narrowing road, disillusionment can give way to despair. When the last nail is lost, and the cultural path ahead seems impassable, many begin to wonder not only where to stand, but whether they can stand at all.

Christians may soon be marginalized, cast aside either as harmless relics or persecuted threats. So, what do we do about all this? That's the question.

The best answer is to say that facing down the realities I've just described demands courage. I made a similar statement during an interview with the *Friends for Life* podcast on KFUO in St. Louis. There, I emphasized staying informed about one's community only matters if it is joined to the courage to act.[13] Awareness without action is inert. But let's be honest: Anyone can prattle on about courage. Real courage—Christian courage—is conditional. It isn't something conjured from the ether or the self. Courage—the kind that truly lives and dies for something—only becomes genuine when it's tethered to objective truth. Living and dying for a lie is not courage. It's foolishness masquerading as bravery.

Foolishness parades itself as boldness when it touts confused sexuality in defiance of natural law. Foolishness thinks shouting "My body, my choice!" at a pro-life rally is brave. It believes canceling someone for expressing disagreement is a virtuous stand. Foolishness views long-standing creeds and doctrinal confessions as chains to be broken—obstacles to a so-called brave new world.

Let me offer a more nuanced explanation of courage—one aligning with the Christian perspective. As President Matthew Harrison of the Lutheran Church–Missouri Synod once put it, "Courage is fear that has been baptized."[14] That is, it is fear washed in the blood of Christ's righteousness.

I don't know about you, but there are times in my life when my resolve feels flimsy, my courage is minimal, and my strength is depleted. I'll catch myself muttering beneath my breath, "I don't think I can go on." I suspect you've had moments like that too. In those moments, I often remember we human beings are never far from the edge of two paths—two very different characters: Judas and Peter.

Both were disciples. Both betrayed the Lord. Both did so for reasons tied to fear and self-preservation. Judas sold Jesus to His enemies. Peter denied Him, even invoking curses to add credibility to his lies. Both were face-to-face with the same haunting urge: the desire for safety in a hostile world.

Judas looked inward and found only despair. Peter looked to Jesus, and there he was restored. He was welcomed back into the brotherhood, his trust now placed not in himself but in the One whose love was greater than his failure.

I find myself, again and again, in places where the darkness swirls and the headwinds howl. I stand at the crossroads of perseverance or forfeit. But by God's grace, and through the eyes of faith, I look past myself and see Jesus. That's when things come into focus. That's when perseverance becomes not only possible but inevitable.

I recall a time when I was preparing to preach on the Good Shepherd text from John 10:11–16. I turned the text inward, toward myself, and what I saw was profoundly humbling. I saw the image Christ painted—not of some distant, pristine shepherd but of one in the trenches, knee-deep in the mud of my unworthiness. I saw the only One who could truly look upon me in my dreadful, filthy, ungrateful, wandering condition and still be willing to lay down His life for me. And not just once but every day—tucking me into His arm, warding off the circling wolves.

That Gospel changes me. It changes my resolve. I become less concerned about what I might be walking into and more focused on simply being faithful to the One who is unfailingly faithful to me, no matter how insignificant my words or deeds may seem.

In short, I've learned—and I'm still learning—for the Christian, courage doesn't originate from within. And I'm reminded I have no business pointing at someone in a congregation and telling them to muster up the courage and get to work. That kind of self-stirred courage is only foolishness in disguise.

Genuine courage—the kind we actually need—is external in origin. It comes from outside us. It is given and sustained by the Gospel. It's found in staying close to Jesus through His Word and sacraments, through the preaching and teaching of God's Word. When a Christian abides there, courage and faith become interchangeable. And as they unite, they produce the capacity to move forward—even when forward seems futile.

Why? Because our eyes are no longer fixed on our own futility. They are fixed on the One who is not only the Good Shepherd but also the Pantocrator—the One who rules all things, who will come again in glory to judge the living and the dead, and whose kingdom will have no end.

Yes, like many of you, I still say from time to time, "I can't go on." But the Gospel answers back with unflinching power: "Yes, you can. Look—there's Jesus. Do you see His cross? Do you see His empty tomb? Behold, He has already carved a way through. The enemies remain, and they are fierce, but He has proven them to be weaker. So, fall in behind Him. Follow. Carry your cross. Use the gifts He's given you. Don't worry about winning. Concern yourself with being faithful, knowing He has you—completely, eternally, and perfectly—in His plentiful care."

The Republican Party's slow unraveling is not just a political phenomenon. It is the inevitable fruit of a deeper spiritual disease—one that transcends party lines and infects every human heart: the worship of the self. At the heart of every political compromise lies a more fundamental theological error. To understand how we arrived here—and what we must resist—we need to step back from politics and examine the spiritual posture defining this cultural moment.

One of the more tragic ironies of our cultural moment is children, by nature, are far better truth-receivers than adults. They do not come to the world armed with ideological frameworks or self-protective narratives. Their understanding is still under construction, which is precisely what makes them moldable by truth. They see what is and, more often than not, call it what it is. Children possess an instinctive honesty that adults, through years of conditioning, argument, and self-justification, tend to lose.

Jesus affirmed as much when He said, "Whoever humbles himself like this child is the greatest in the kingdom of heaven" (Matt. 18:4). He wasn't calling attention to childish ignorance or naivety but to a spiritual disposition standing ready to be taught. A child does not pretend to have all the answers. A child does not fear being corrected. A child expects truth to come from outside themselves—and trusts the one who gives it.

That humility isn't just moral; it's epistemological.[15] It's not merely about being "nice" or "teachable." It's about submitting one's understanding to something greater than the self. It's about being formed by the Word, not forming the Word into a reflection of personal desire. This distinction is no small matter. It sits at the heart of what it means to believe.

Children are naturally open to truth. Adults are naturally hostile to it. This hostility is learned. It develops slowly through repeated acts of self-deception and cultural catechesis. Adults become experts in justifying what they want, twisting what is clear, and rejecting what is inconvenient. It is not that they cannot see the truth. It is that they will not. Their resistance is not intellectual; it is spiritual.

This is why radical individualism is so fundamentally absurd. It lionizes the adult mind as sovereign and treats the self as the final arbiter of meaning. In doing so, it elevates the most arrogant posture imaginable—self-rule over even the most obvious realities.

It trains adults to believe the self is the sole authority over what is real. Radical individualism flatters the ego into believing nothing is more sacred than personal preference. "If I feel it, it is so." That is its creed. Biology, history, Scripture—these must all bow to the self's sense of identity and desire. This worldview unravels any shared understanding of truth and undermines society's most basic agreements about what is.

But children don't operate that way. They adapt to what is. Their minds are still flexible. Their categories are not yet ossified. And so, they receive rather than resist. They do not assert their will over facts. They adjust to reality rather than commanding reality to adjust to them. They receive information, and if it doesn't fit their current understanding, they adjust. They build new categories rather than force facts into old ones.

This is what makes children naturally better exegetes than most adults. When they encounter something new or unfamiliar, their first instinct is to ask, not argue. They assume what they are seeing must be understood on its own terms—not warped to suit preexisting opinions. This is a virtue of both curiosity and humility, a virtue modern culture has nearly extinguished in adults.

I'm sure plenty of parents have seen this happen in real-time. For example, a child sees a dog for the first time. He learns to call it "dog." He sees a snake. It's far different from a dog, so he asks what it is. He learns to call it "snake." But then he sees a squirrel. It looks absolutely nothing like a snake, so he knows it isn't one. That's easy. And it's little more than honest observation. Still, his categories are limited. He has to put the squirrel somewhere into his knowledge base. Therefore, he notices its fur. He sees it has a tail. He watches it run across the yard on four legs. Only knowing dogs and snakes, he points proudly and says, "Momma! Dog!" When the mom clarifies it's a squirrel, the child creates a new category based on fact. He doesn't argue with his mom about the squirrel's dogness, protesting or accusing her of intolerance. He doesn't try to convince her the squirrel is really a dog trapped in a squirrel's body. It's simply not a dog. It's a squirrel. The facts change the child. He adapts. Piaget showed that adaptation is innate to child development, being more so relative to natural law. Every normal human child does it instinctually.[16]

Piaget demonstrated that there are only two reasons a child would deliberately think a squirrel is a dog. The first is if he was completely ignorant of squirrels, and because he is attempting to grow and learn in truth, he adds the animal to the only available categories he knows. The second is if an adult lied to him, interrupting the child's ordinary course of development and confusing the categories.

This is radical individualism.

Radical individualism insists that truth conform to the self. And this is where silliness turns sinister. What begins as a celebration of "authenticity" soon morphs into a refusal to recognize any truth external to one's feelings. In such a world, anyone who insists on categories rooted in creation—such as male and female, or right and wrong—is cast as an oppressor. The self reigns supreme and dissent becomes heresy.

Theologically, this inversion is not neutral. It's the sin nature at work. The impulse to redefine is not merely psychological. It is spiritual rebellion. The first lie ever told was a question aimed at God's authority: "Did God really say . . . ?" (Gen. 3:1). That lie still echoes today—sometimes from pulpits, often from classrooms and courtrooms, and always from within. Why? Because the sin nature refuses to be shaped by truth. It demands truth to be shaped by the self. It does not want God to speak. It wants to speak in God's place. It does not want to listen. It wants to declare.

That's the essence of radical individualism. And it's why it ultimately collapses into incoherence. The house of the self cannot bear the weight of being the universe. It eventually folds in on itself, unable to sustain the demands of its own sovereignty. A squirrel will never be a dog. A man will never be a woman. A lie will never become true no matter how sincerely believed. These are not statements of cruelty. They are statements of love—because they are statements of reality. Denying them does not liberate. It deceives.

Christians are called to something very different: a faith that receives truth with humility. We are not called to invent truth but to submit to it. Not to express ourselves but to die to ourselves. To be re-formed, not to self-affirm. The former leads to life. The latter leads only to deeper darkness. In this age of self-deification, the true Church must remember which is which.

Chapter 16

The Courage to Speak Anyway

Is there a colder sensation than entering a room of people and knowing you were already unwelcome before you walked through the door? It's a unique feeling—unsettling, isolating—that most hope to avoid. The world, by its very nature, hardwires us to gravitate toward places where we are celebrated rather than rejected—or, at the very least, tolerated. For this reason, many instinctively choose to sidestep circumstances where the hope of belonging is little more than a misplaced assumption.

Naming this experience veers a bit from the central matter I have in mind and yet it remains connected. In one sense, my aim here is simply to acknowledge that few things shake the soul quite like returning to a place that once felt like home, only to discover it does no longer. The furnishings may remain unchanged, the people familiar, but something foundational has shifted, leaving the returning heart unmoored.

As I reflect on this, my thoughts are drawn to the Lord's words in Luke 4:24—words also appearing in Matthew 13:53–58 and Mark 6:1–6: "Truly, I say to you, no prophet is acceptable in his hometown." While pastors will readily resonate with this verse, I believe it reaches deeper than vocational experience. It offers a profound commentary on human nature itself—our tendency to dismiss without pause what we think we already understand, especially when it comes to the people we've known.

Jesus experienced this dismissal firsthand. When He returned to His hometown of Nazareth, He was met not with celebration but with suspicion and scorn. Those who watched Him grow, who remembered Him as Mary's son and Joseph's apprentice, could not reconcile the boy they once knew with the man now proclaiming the Kingdom of God. Their familiarity with His past clouded their vision in the present. They were blind to His identity and deaf to His truth—not because His message lacked substance, but because it came from someone they believed they had already figured out.[1]

Have you ever tried to warn someone of impending danger, only to have your concern rejected outright—perhaps even interpreted as arrogance or insult? I have. And when I reflect more deeply on Luke 4, I find comfort in the company it offers. After Jesus's sermon in the synagogue, the Gospel account tells us: "When they heard these things, all in the synagogue were filled with wrath. And they rose up and drove him out of the town and brought him to the brow of the hill on which their town was built, so that they could throw him down the cliff. But passing through their midst, he went away" (vv. 28–30).

One of the most sobering elements of this narrative is Jesus "went away." The biblical record offers no evidence He ever returned to Nazareth. Instead, He turned His attention to Capernaum and to the towns and villages beyond, spreading the Gospel to people who might receive it. Still, before departing, He tried. He knew what was likely to happen. He understood the proverb about prophets and hometowns. Yet He went. He spoke. He loved them enough to risk their wrath.[2]

This, I think, is the very crux of what I'm wrestling with in this chapter.

It is right to care for one's own. Indeed, we should be ready and willing to speak the truth not only to strangers but to those closest to us. Still, faithfulness does not demand we remain indefinitely where we are rejected. There comes a time, as Jesus taught, to shake the dust from our feet and move on—to invest in hearts made of better soil (Matt. 10:14; Luke 8:15).

In Luke 8, Jesus shares the parable of the sower, a story about scattering seed across different types of terrain. Immediately following this, He gives a striking warning: "Take care then how you hear, for to the one who has, more will be given, and from the one who has not, even what he thinks that he has will be taken away" (v. 18). The message is clear: The soil matters. So does the willingness to listen and receive.

Seen from a wider perspective, these stories offer more than just historical insight. They extend a divine invitation to reconsider how we measure success. Rejection—even when it comes from those who once embraced us—should never serve as a deterrent to truth-telling. Jesus did not center His ministry in Nazareth. He did not skip it, either. He spoke with clarity and conviction, even knowing what was coming. In this, we are reminded that while rejection may alter our path, it should not define our purpose.

What matters is doing what is faithful, discerning the proper time to remain and the proper time to depart. Sometimes a closed door is not a defeat—it is God's redirection toward soil more ready for cultivation. The apostle Paul's experience in Acts 16:6–10 affirms this reality. Prevented from entering certain regions, he was instead called by vision to Macedonia. The redirection was not a loss but a divine appointment.

Paul, like his Lord, understood rejection. He bore it often. And yet he could write with confident humility: "Am I seeking the approval of man, or of God? Or am I trying to please man? If I were still trying to please man, I would not be a servant of Christ" (Gal. 1:10). Paul's commitment was not contingent upon acceptance. His compass was calibrated to faithfulness. No other standard held sway.

These truths belong in the public square.

The temptation to avoid hard conversations in the civic realm is as real as the instinct to avoid conflict in our families or hometowns. And yet, if the Church refuses to speak where she is unwelcome, she forfeits a core component of her identity. The call to proclaim truth in love—to confront sin, to defend life, to untangle confusion, to uphold God's design for society—extends into city halls, legislative chambers, courtrooms, school board meetings, and every public domain where Christian conscience is increasingly unwelcome.[3]

When Christians step into these arenas, they experience what Jesus likely experienced in Nazareth. Eyes roll. Doors close. Accusations fly. "Who are you to speak this way?" "Didn't you used to be one of us?" "Keep your religious opinions to yourself." These reactions are designed to silence and shame and to make the faithful feel out of place in a world they share with everyone else. But remember: It is not acceptance that validates the message. It is its alignment with Christ. And it is not comfort that signals success but courage rooted in truth.

For those who know what it feels like to be unwelcome—to enter a space and sense they are already judged, already disqualified, already dismissed—this truth can be deeply liberating. I speak from experience. I've walked into rooms I knew would not be hospitable. I've sat across from people who, before I even opened my mouth, had already closed their hearts. Still, I went. Still, I spoke. And, in time, I've learned that some of those moments bore fruit—years later, in unexpected ways. Others did not. But in either case, the outcome was never mine to produce. The Lord never asked for results. He desires faithfulness.[4]

Faithfulness—not visible success—is the unchanging goal. And more often than not, faithfulness means laboring without immediate evidence that your work is having any effect. It means planting seeds you may never see bloom. It means trusting God, who sees the unseen, will use every effort for His purposes—even those efforts that seem to vanish into barren ground. This is no easy task. At times, it can feel like a hard truth to accept. But it is a truth we can swallow by faith. And once swallowed, it nourishes the soul for the long road ahead.

As Christians—especially pastors and leaders—we must remember our call into the public square will sometimes yield rejection, not applause, even from our own congregations.[5] But even in rejection, there is fruit. Sometimes it is borne in the hearer. At other times, it is borne in the speaker. Either way, the Kingdom advances—not through popularity or consensus but through truth proclaimed and lived, even when unwelcome.

Chapter 17

INVALIDATE THE LIE

I once asked the students in my 7th and 8th grade religion class to describe the behaviors among friends that hurt them most deeply. Their responses were both honest and insightful. Some mentioned cliquish behavior. Others pointed to cruel or mocking words. One student, struggling to define what she was feeling, described a kind of self-absorbed behavior leaving her feeling invisible and diminished. I gave her the word she was searching for: narcissism.

In turn, the students asked me the same question. I told them I despise lying.[1] You can mock me, belittle me, even curse the day I was born—plenty have done so. And strangely, some of those friendships have endured. They stand now as testaments to God's grace and the mysterious way He mends the broken. But lying—intentional deception—is different. It's the one act, for me, that shifts a relationship in often irreparable ways. It's not that forgiveness won't eventually prevail. It must. And it will. We can even remain friends. But from my vantage point, we'll become distant friends. Something sacred is lost in the exchange.

Of course, I say this as someone just as guilty of deceit as the next person. In the mind's eye, I sometimes picture a singular door—ancient, ominous—marked by a scorched placard bearing three letters: L, I, and E. It was the devil who first unlocked that dreadful door in Eden. Humanity turned the knob and sin stepped through. Not a few of us but *all* of us have since been infected. If you find this hard to believe, consider the observation of eighteenth-century philosopher Denis Diderot: "We swallow greedily any lie that flatters us, but we sip only little by little at a truth we find bitter."[2]

Truth is bitter to sin. It prefers to gulp from deceit.

And God, conversely, despises untruth. He rejects it so thoroughly that He has embedded truth into the very fabric of created reality. His natural law is not subject to the whims of cultural redefinition. It is unbending, unbreachable. It can be misunderstood, yes—but it cannot lie. A man may deceive himself in countless ways. He may believe himself to be a woman. But he will never *be* a woman. A man may believe he is a bird, but if he leaps from a rooftop without heeding the mechanics ordained by natural law, he won't fly—he'll die. Natural law will judge, convict, and sentence all its offenders.

This is where Christian witness matters—not merely in private piety but in public confession. These truths are not only personal—they're *civic*. They frame our laws, our norms, and our liberties. To accept a lie at the cultural level is to legislate confusion and codify injustice. Religious liberty is hollow if divorced from the courage to speak the truth publicly.

Truths like these are all around us. The only real way to obscure them is through lies. And yet, no matter how obscured, truth will eventually meet the lie. It always does. From a human perspective, I suspect one of two outcomes arises when that meeting occurs. Either the lie is corrected by truth and the travelers on that path are spared, or the travelers bent on self-worship choose destruction over surrender. In either case, the nature of the lie is revealed—it exerts a persuasive sway not to be underestimated.

I've written in other places how I sometimes spell "sin" with a capital "S." It's because I believe sin is a serious matter. It's a very real, very active power in the world—one meriting special attention. If sin were inconsequential, there would have been no need for the divine Son of God to wage war against it. Perhaps

I should begin capitalizing the word "lie" as well. Lying is not some insignificant vice. Mark Twain captured this well when he said, "One of the most striking differences between a cat and a lie is that a cat has only nine lives."[3] Lies are endlessly replicable. If not stopped, they only multiply. And when believed, their trajectory skyrockets toward destruction.

Just look around. Horrific untruths are being perpetuated and believed. These untruths, like a blackened tsunami, are sweeping across the globe, drowning lives in shadow. A pastor and friend in Canada told me his son was arrested and fined $10,000 for reading the Bible and praying across the street from an LGBTQ demonstration.[4] I read about an after-school satanic club starting in various elementary schools.[5] I read another story about a drag show in an elementary school.[6]

Each of these examples reveals something about our cultural moment: The lie has not only been believed but publicly institutionalized. What once dwelled in moral shadows now parades down Main Street with legal protection and taxpayer funding. This is what happens when religious liberty is recast as private feeling rather than public fidelity. It is not merely Christians who are free to believe as they wish. It is we who are called to say what is true, even when it collides with what the world demands we say instead.

Should we be surprised by these things? Perhaps. But if you are, it likely means you haven't been paying attention. Though I doubt many Michiganders are shocked. Attorney General Dana Nessel once gave a speech expressing a desire to see drag queens in every Michigan school.[7] This state isn't just sipping from deceit. It's chugging.

And by the way, if you're a Michigander who voted for Nessel, you're among the foolhardy I mentioned earlier. Like it or not, you are cheering for the tsunami. And let's be clear: In the public square, your vote *is* your voice. It's your confession. It's your cultural engagement, whether faithful or faithless.

So, what are we to do?

I have a two-step answer. But I'll warn you: The answer is jarring—perhaps even offensive. Why? Because it demands courage and conviction—virtues often in short supply in a self-preserving and radically individualized culture like ours.

Step one is the admission that truth exists—it is knowable, and it applies to everyone, not just a select few. You do not have your own truth. No one does. The sooner you accept this, the better. Religious liberty means nothing if it's decoupled from reality. We are not free to invent lies and call them righteousness.

Step two, a daily and far more difficult step is to live according to truth and be ever ready to invalidate untruth. This second step almost guarantees discomfort and division. But it must be taken. Let me offer a personal example.

Earlier this week, I took an online questionnaire. Right at the beginning, it asked for my gender, offering a long list of options. Thankfully, "male" was one of them, and I selected it. Then I noticed a small comment box for elaboration. I typed, "There are only two genders, male and female." That comment may mean very little to the company collecting my data. But the opportunity to invalidate a lie was there, and though small, I took it.

That, too, is public square engagement. It may seem trivial, but it's a seed. And when millions of such seeds are planted, the lie begins to lose ground.

Of course, invalidating lies becomes significantly harder when it involves real people—family, friends, even fellow Christians. Still, it must be done. For instance, when you're invited to your homosexual niece's wedding, you must decline the invitation. If you go, telling yourself it's to maintain family peace, know this: Your presence will be perceived as approval unless you make your objection known publicly. Even as you stay home, do not lie and say you had prior plans. Speak the truth. Invalidate the lie of same-sex marriage.

Or when your son chooses to pursue a healthcare career that will inevitably involve abortion, you must withdraw all material support. Don't cop out with vague platitudes like, "It's time you make your own way." Speak the truth. Invalidate the lie abortion that is anything but murder.

Or if your pastor begins to espouse the doctrines of Critical Race Theory or DEI (Diversity, Equity, and Inclusion), you must confront him. Admonish him. Refute the error. Say clearly why.

This is what it means to be the Church militant in the age of confusion. Until our allegiance to Christ eclipses our allegiance to people, the lie will continue to gain ground, and its advance will leave devastation in its path. That devastation will not stop at the courts, schools, and legislatures. It will seep into our churches too. In fact, the overwhelming silence from so many pulpits affirms it already has.

Take a moment and look at Mark 15:43. You'll find Joseph of Arimathea, a quiet believer and "a respected member of the ruling council." In other words, he lived among the Pharisees—Christ's most ardent enemies. According to John 19:38, Joseph kept his faith hidden "for fear of the Jews." His concern for his colleagues outweighed his allegiance to his Lord.

But then the Lord died. Joseph saw it. Mark records that Joseph "took courage and went to Pilate and asked for the body of Jesus" (15:43). Validating the lie that Jesus was a charlatan with his silence was no longer an option for Joseph. He took courage. This courage became action, forever changing Joseph's public standing before friends and foes. It was Chrysostom who wrote, "This was Joseph, who had been concealing his discipleship. Now he became very bold, after the death of Christ. For neither was he an obscure person nor unnoticed. He was one of the council, and highly distinguished, and as we see, courageous. For he exposed himself to death, taking upon himself the enmity of all by his affection to Jesus."[8]

That is the kind of courage it takes to invalidate lies.

And here's the remarkable truth: For all the fear the world attempts to instill in us, Christ has promised that such courage will be given to His people. He said, "You will be dragged before governors and kings for my sake, to bear witness before them and the Gentiles" (Matt. 10:18). And when that terrifying moment arrives? "The Holy Spirit will teach you in that very hour what you ought to say" (Luke 12:12).

So, listen to Jesus. Trust Him. Take a cue from Joseph. Dig into the courage that is already yours by faith. Meet the lie wherever you find it. Confront it not with rage or arrogance but with the love of Christ. Speak the truth. Hold the line. Your witness isn't just personal. It is public. And it is desperately needed.

It won't be easy. But then again, few things worth doing ever are.

❧

Chapter 18

A Leaf on the Tree

I have a story to tell you. It's a personal one, and I hope you'll allow me a little more of your time than usual to tell it well. To begin, let me direct your attention to the portrait hanging above the desk in the guest room of our basement. It displays a fabric rendition of the Thoma coat of arms. Nestled beside the emblem, framed within the same display, is a modest but detailed recounting of ancestral history.

Now, I should preface by noting in today's world, it doesn't take much to discover your family name supposedly has a coat of arms. A simple internet search will turn up one ready for download—for a nominal fee, of course. We live in a time where everyone is important, and so, it seems, everyone gets a trophy. So, for $29.99, here's your "ancient" coat of arms.

I believe ours is authentic. Over the years, I've come across versions of it in various historical archives. Interestingly, there are at least two recorded variants—one featuring a duck on its shield and the other without. Apparently, this was not uncommon. During lunch yesterday, I explained to my wife, Jennifer, how surnames often have variants, which meant the coats of arms would reflect those differences. In the case of the duck, I discovered it symbolized resourcefulness. If a duck appeared on a family's coat of arms, it meant the family proved themselves clever, willing to outwit and defeat their foes through ingenuity.

For the record, Jennifer and I acquired our framed portrait shortly after we were married, which means it has been hanging in our home since the mid-1990s. Whether or not the coat of arms is fully traceable to the eleventh century, it's certainly "ancient" in our house by modern standards. Still, the historical information beside it is accurate. I've conducted research over the years, searching out each detail and validating it through corroborating sources, which often led me even deeper into our family's story.

I learned, for example, the Thoma surname was first recorded in 1100 and was ascribed to a Roman Catholic priest. Like most surnames, variations soon followed. In 1252, there was a Henneko filius (son of) Thome living in Hamburg, Germany. Later, in 1413, a man named Tilusch Thoman appeared in the records of Magdeburg, noted as a brewer of beer. Considering my appreciation for distilled spirits, I wasn't the least bit surprised alcohol made an appearance somewhere in our heritage.

Continuing through the centuries, the first recorded appearance of a Thoma in America was in 1761. Durst Thoma arrived from Germany and settled in the remote Pennsylvania countryside. A few years later, in 1764, one of Durst's sons, Johann Philip Thoma, made his home in Philadelphia. That particular detail caught my attention, given the city's historical significance during the Revolutionary period. It leaves me wondering whether Johann had some part in America's fight for independence. With the same kind of instinct I have for public engagement, it wouldn't surprise me if there were a genetic predisposition nudging him in that direction. Did he settle in Philadelphia to join the swelling ranks of those preparing to confront tyranny? Perhaps I'll pursue that rabbit trail more seriously one day.

Still, all of this is only background. It leads to the true heart of the story I want to share.

As you might have guessed, the Thoma name is of thoroughly German origin. Along the ancestral trail, I discovered a few prominent bearers of the name—Roman Catholic archbishops, naval captains, and other notable figures from history. But among the most compelling of them all, and perhaps the most unsung, was a Nazi soldier.

Now, before you draw the wrong conclusion, let me explain.

Busso Thoma (October 31, 1899–January 23, 1945) first served in the Imperial German Infantry during World War I. After the war, he became a salesman. But in time, he returned to military service, rejoining the Army during World War II as a major in the Oberkommando des Heeres—the High Command of the Nazi Army. In 1941, Busso met Hermann Kaiser, a staff captain responsible for maintaining the war diaries for Friedrich Fromm, commander-in-chief of the Reserve Army. Through that relationship, Busso became connected to the German resistance. Eventually, he joined the effort led by Colonel Claus von Stauffenberg and became an essential participant in the assassination attempt on Adolf Hitler—an operation code-named Valkyrie.[1]

Yes, a Thoma stood against Hitler.

The short version of Operation Valkyrie is this: On July 20, 1944, Stauffenberg placed a briefcase bomb near Hitler inside the *Wolfsschanze* (Wolf's Lair) command bunker in East Prussia. When the bomb detonated, killing three high-ranking Nazi officers, Busso was already stationed at Bendler Block, the Army High Command headquarters in Berlin. There, as a commanding officer, he helped orchestrate the resistance response, anticipating the Reich Security forces would be dispatched to reclaim the building.[2]

Tragically, the attempt on Hitler's life failed. Despite the deaths of three monstrous Nazi commanders, Hitler survived. In Berlin, just as the conspirators predicted, the Reich's security forces descended upon Bendler Block. A firefight ensued, and Busso was captured.[3]

Remarkably, Busso managed to escape. A demonstration of his duck-like resourcefulness, perhaps? Still, his freedom was brief. Two months later, the Gestapo caught up to him. Brought before the notorious *Volksgerichtshof* (People's Court), Busso boldly confessed to his role in the plot. On January 17, 1945, he was sentenced to death as a capital conspirator. Six days later, on January 23, he was executed by hanging at Plötzensee Prison in Berlin.[4]

I shared much of this with my daughter, Madeline, a few weeks ago. She listened intently and, apart from asking about the battle at Bendler Block and Busso's defiance in court, she wondered whether Busso ever knew Dietrich Bonhoeffer. That's a good question. While I can't say for certain, I've never come across Busso's name in my studies of Bonhoeffer, even during the deep dives of my doctoral work. Still, as the saying goes, absence of evidence is not evidence of absence. Bonhoeffer was deeply influential within the German resistance. As a German Lutheran, Busso may well have heard him preach or speak. It's possible. One day, I may chase that line of inquiry further.

For now, I left the conversation with Madeline having confirmed two thoughts.

First, based on what we know of our own family, it should come as no surprise that a Thoma was involved in Operation Valkyrie. There are several branches of the Thoma family tree, but if I may speak specifically for our branch here in Michigan, we are not the sort to polish beliefs with words and leave them on a shelf. We put feet to our faith. We engage. And sometimes that gets us into trouble. My kids do it in school, whether they're addressing their peers or their teachers. My wife, Jennifer, has the same spirit. And frankly, even apart from my current work in the public square, I suspect, had I been a pastor in Nazi Germany, I would have found my way to a jail cell sooner than later. I can't seem to keep my typing fingers still or my mouth shut in places where truth needs defending.

Second, as significant as Busso's efforts were, he remains unsung. He acted decisively when action was required. He demonstrated remarkable courage. But there are no statues of him. The monument at Bendler Block depicts Stauffenberg. The plaque beneath it offers only a general remembrance for the unnamed others who died in the cause.[5] I understand why. Stauffenberg was the architect of the plan. Still, many others, including Busso, gave their lives trying to rid the world of the Nazi scourge.[6] Like the millions who died during the war, most will remain unknown to history.

And that, I believe, is a lesson in itself.

If someone is only willing to serve because they expect recognition, they've missed the point entirely. I doubt Stauffenberg expected a statue. I'm confident Busso didn't. True servants—those who stand up in decisive moments—rarely act for the sake of personal glory. In fact, those in it for glory are often the most dangerous to any cause. But those who act for the sake of others, regardless of the cost, these are the ones who do the most good. They give entirely of themselves not for gain but because it is right. They face the dragons others fear. They speak the truth, engage the battle, and embrace the consequences because they know others will suffer if they do not.

I wouldn't expect you to have heard of Busso Thoma. I hadn't, either, until a few years ago. He's a leaf on one of the branches of the Thoma family tree. But his story, like many others, has remained buried beneath the weight of history. And yet, for those of us looking at this world through the lens of the Gospel, there's something profoundly Christlike in what he did.

Everything I've described so far can be located perfectly in Jesus Christ. He is the definitive emblem of selfless love. He came to serve, not to be served, and to give His life as a ransom (Matt. 20:28). He said plainly, "Greater love has no one than this, that someone lay down his life for his friends" (John 15:13). And we are those friends. He laid down His life for us so we might walk free from sin's tyranny.

From my experience, Christians who truly grasp this live accordingly. They understand reward doesn't come through monuments, medals, or having a church wing named after them. Their reward is found in Christ alone—in the undeserved salvation purchased by His blood. Anchored in the Gospel, they imitate their Savior (1 Cor. 11:1; Eph. 5:1–12). They endure hardship. They speak the truth in dark places. And whether they succeed or fail, whether they live to see the fruit or die in obscurity, they know their labor is never in vain (1 Cor. 15:58).

I intend to remember Busso each year on January 23. I've already added him to the list of people I want to meet when I finally enter eternal glory. Maybe cousin Tilusch will be there too, ready to mix and pour heaven's finest drams. And perhaps Johann will join us to share why he chose Philadelphia. I look forward to asking.

Conclusion

The Unyielding Triumph of the Risen Christ

The resurrection of Jesus Christ stands as the cornerstone of Christian faith, a reality so undeniable that it reshapes the course of history and the contours of human existence.

The tomb is empty. Christ is alive. He appeared to His disciples in the flesh, not as a specter or illusion but as a living, breathing Savior. They saw Him, touched the scars of His crucifixion, shared meals with Him, and marveled at the vibrancy of His restored life. There was no scent of decay. His skin was not pale. His limbs moved with purpose. His eyes shone with grace. His voice, steady and certain, spoke words of eternal promise—of peace.

For Christians, this is no mere story. And it certainly is more than a historical fact.[1] It is the defining truth anchoring the Christian confession and fueling the courage to proclaim it.

Still, there is the seemingly never-ending parade of cynics, in the past and present. Nevertheless, Christ's resurrection is not a myth crafted by desperate followers, as these enemies claim.[2] The accusations of stolen bodies or fabricated tales crumbled under the weight of countless testimonies—men and women who saw Him, spoke with Him, and were transformed by Him.[3] Even Saul of Tarsus, a fierce opponent of the early Church, became Paul, an apostle of Christ, after encountering the risen Lord on the road to Damascus. This singular event turned an ardent persecutor into a devoted apostle, a skeptic into a servant, proving no heart is beyond the reach of the risen Christ's grace.

The Lord's most enthusiastic enemies—from the Pharisees to the Roman authorities—anticipated He would simply fade into obscurity. They believed time would erode the fervor of Christ's followers, the passage of years would bury all of it. A handful of backwater nobodies, they reasoned, could not sustain a religion against the might of empires or the scorn of cultured elites.

Yet, here we stand, centuries later, on every continent, in lands where faith flourishes and in domains where it is fiercely opposed.[4] Christians across the globe unite in the triumphant cry: "Christ is risen! He is risen, indeed! Alleluia!" This proclamation echoes through time, undeterred by persecution, skepticism, or cultural shifts.[5] It is a song even the most ardent adversaries—whether in this life or at the final judgment—will one day join, as Scripture promises every knee will bow and every tongue confess the lordship of Christ (Phil. 2:10).

I'm reminded of Emperor Julian the Apostate, who, despite his Christian upbringing, sought to revive Roman paganism and extinguish the faith. In his brief reign (AD 361–363), he wielded the full authority of the empire to marginalize Christians, stripping their rights and promoting a rival religion.[6] Yet, his efforts were futile. On his deathbed, wounded and defeated, he uttered his final, begrudging confession: *"Vicisti, Galilaee"*—"You have conquered, O Galilean."[7] Julian's failure is but one chapter in a long history of opposition to the Gospel, from the Sanhedrin to the Caesars, from Enlightenment skeptics to modern secularists. Each has tried to silence the message of Christ, and each has found it impervious, a juggernaut moving inexorably across the landscape of human existence.[8]

This unyielding resilience speaks directly to the themes explored in this book. The Great Decline, as some have termed it, reflects the waning influence of Christianity in contemporary America, a phenomenon marked by radical individualism, clergy and parishioner disengagement, and a dissonance between faith and deeds. Yet, the resurrection assures us the Church's mission endures, even in seasons of ebb.

The historical survey of early America revealed a nation shaped by Christian convictions, where clergy and laity alike engaged the public square with courage, grounded in biblical precedents and a robust understanding of the Two Kingdoms doctrine. The distinctions between separationism and accommodationism, which have been examined, test the Church's ability to navigate and maintain its role in a pluralistic society. But regardless the topics considered throughout all this, the empty tomb is the best reminder that no cultural tide, no political edict, no societal pressure can ultimately prevail against the Church that Christ promised to sustain (Matt. 16:18).

Besides, the risen Christ warned that faith would not always flourish. He commissioned His disciples to reach into the world for others (Matt. 28:19). He did this, having already questioned whether He would find faith on earth at His return (Luke 18:8). These words are both sobering and comforting. They acknowledge the reality of decline—moments when the Church seems to falter, when courage wanes, when conviction is diluted by compromise or apathy. Yet, they also affirm the certainty of the Gospel's endurance.

Jesus promised He would never leave nor forsake His people, He would be with them always, even to the end of the age (Matt. 28:20). In an America where the snuffing out of Christian influence is in an unprecedented upsurge, this promise does not falter or fade. It remains. Faithful churches continue to proclaim the Good News of salvation through faith in Christ, undeterred by hostility or indifference. The Galilean's victory is not contingent on cultural approval or institutional power. It is secured by His resurrection, a fact no force in heaven or on earth can undo.

Reflecting on what has been observed and identified throughout this volume, I'm comfortable in drawing to a close, knowing each challenge has been met with an encouraging word toward renewed commitment—to be who God has made you to be. The resurrection is the certificate of this Christian identity. With it in both hand and heart, Christians go into the world more than aware the Lord we claim is by no means a distant figure. Jesus is present. He is leading. He is equipping His people to face the complexities of a rapidly changing world. He is steadying us to stand firm, no matter where we are or what we are doing, with the same conviction that transformed fishermen into apostles and persecutors into martyrs.

May you, dear reader, be fortified by the Holy Spirit to rejoice in the victory of the One who gave His life on the cross and took it up again in conquering might. His resurrection is your assurance the Gospel will continue to advance, unbroken and unstoppable, across all landscapes—created and uncreated—until the day of His return.

Indeed, Christ is risen! He is risen, indeed! Alleluia!

❧

Postscript

Life in a Post–Charlie Kirk World

The body of this volume was written and concluded in May of 2025. And then September 10 arrived.

A friend, upon hearing the news of Charlie Kirk's assassination, wrote on social media, "Something's gotta change."

Charlie—a husband, father, and brother in Christ—was dead because someone thought a bullet was the answer to a message he didn't want to hear. He was shot not while hiding in the shadows, not while plotting violence, but while doing what he always did best. Charlie was standing openly in the public square, speaking of truth, speaking of faith—heralding freedom.

I'll be clear. I was devastated. Not only because Charlie, a personal friend, lost his life, but also because the quietism plaguing the Church required him to be in situations where his life was at stake.

This is to say, he was out and doing what few others would.

Indeed, I catch more flak from clergy than I do from the radicalized left. It's just a fact. And it's troubling. But that's a topic for another book.

In the meantime, what happened to Charlie is not just another headline. It isn't "polarization." This is what happens when years of slander, lawfare, and vilification ripen. Call someone "Hitler" often enough, and eventually someone will feel justified in pulling a trigger. And here we are.

A congressman nearly dies at baseball practice under a spray of bullets. A man with fourteen mugshots walks free until he murders a woman on mass transit. President Trump has already survived two assassination attempts in just over a year.

And now Charlie.

Each time, the chorus from the media and the elites is the same: silence. Crickets. Hand-wringing about "tone" or "polarization," as if it's all just a misunderstanding between two equal sides. But it's not. One side is being silenced by intimidation, deplatforming, lawfare, and now the ever-present threat of violence. The message is unmistakable. If you speak the truth too boldly, if you stand for faith and freedom too firmly, there will be a price.

It's not like we were best friends. Still, I've known Charlie for a while. His life tells the story. He wasn't content to preach to the choir. He went to the places where his message was least welcome—college campuses. He invited disagreement, welcomed debate, and carried himself with cheer and grace even in hostile territory. That's what free speech looks like. That's what commitment looks like. And yet, for daring to speak, he paid the ultimate price.

There is a hard truth America must face. Christians and conservatives are being targeted. Not in whispers but in plain view. Not just with words but with bullets. If you love this country, if you love freedom, if you love the right to speak and worship without fear, you cannot sit idly by—even if your pastor instructs you to.

Get in the game, because you're in it already. If you are a Christian, you are salt and light for a world in dreadful darkness. God made you this. Now, by the power of the Holy Spirit at work within you for faith, go and be it.

There is no retreat. The only response is courage. First, there is the courage to pray without ceasing for Charlie's wife and children. They need the comfort only Christ can give. From there, muster the courage to speak the truth, even if it means losing friends, jobs, or platforms. What we face is bigger than these things. It's bigger than politics. It is nothing less than a spiritual battle against the powers of darkness.

We cannot allow violence to dictate who gets to speak. We cannot allow fear to muzzle truth. If this moment was meant to frighten so many even further into silence, then it must become the very moment we resolve to speak louder, stand firmer, and link arms more tightly than ever before.

Charlie gave much to this nation. He gave his voice, his strength, his passion, his resources. Now, he gave all he had left.

My friend was right. Something has to change. That something is you. Be one who is no longer afraid to call evil what it is. Refuse to be silent. Refuse to bow. Refuse to let evil have the last word.

The Rot of Quietism

Charlie Kirk's courage also exposes a festering wound in the Church. It is something already thoroughly examined in this book: Too many Christians, namely pastors, have fallen silent.

In an age when the wolves howl in the open, the shepherds often retreat into whispers. But why? After years in the trenches, and countless conversations with clergy, I can tell you one fundamental reason.

Silence risks nothing. It doesn't risk the paycheck. It doesn't risk the security. It doesn't risk congregation division. Pastors, called to be guardians of the flock, whether they realize it or not, often hide behind abstractions, clichés, and vague theological "applications" never risking offense. And so, the sheep wander, harassed and helpless (Matt. 9:36), while the shepherds polish their sermons with careful neutrality.

But a little bit of self-reflection and a pastor might realize that silence is not safety. Silence is surrender. Christ did not call His shepherds to surrender to the world's expectations. He called them to surrender to Him. As such, they are made heralds of the Truth. And the Truth, as Charlie reminded us by both word and deed, cannot be divided into harmless categories—one slice for the Gospel, another for politics, another for culture. Truth is whole. Truth is the Good Shepherd—Christ—everything He is.

And so, when the pastors, the undershepherds, refuse to speak, the wolves do not retreat. They advance. They teach the children. They shape the culture—even the Church's culture. They redefine male and female. They catechize the congregation with the liturgies of CRT, DEI, and self-made identity. Neutrality, then, is not polite churchmanship but abdication. The silence of the undershepherds is consent to the wolves.

Jesus warns about the hired hand who sees the wolf coming and flees, proving he cares nothing for the sheep (John 10:12–13). And yet, even as the hired hand remains safely professional and polished, he becomes powerless in his role. Afraid to name the sins devouring the flock, they become content to rely on platitudes, hoping the wolf will be satisfied with someone else's blood.

Maybe Charlie's blood.

This is the shame of Christian quietism.

The pastor's calling is not to build a wall of safety for himself in this world. It is to preach and teach the Gospel in purity and to administer the sacraments according to Christ's command. This is dangerous work because it steers headlong into everything Satan would prefer for the sheep. For one, he would have the sheep slow-boiled into being comfortable in destruction. And yet, to protect the sheep, a pastor is to afflict the comfortable. To preach Christ crucified means to name the sins for which Jesus died, not to blur them into generic "brokenness" easily disregarded. Sheep need precision. Sheep need clarity. Sheep need truth. Sheep need undershepherds who will lift the rod and staff against the enemy, not hide them in quietism's sheath.

I know it's scary. Still, the sheep need watchmen who will not hold their peace, day or night (Isa. 62:6). Silence is simply not an option. Neither is neutrality. For example, pastors must be willing to inform their people how electing candidates who advocate for ideologies contrary to Christ's will means taking a grave step away from the Savior. And then they need to name the candidates who do this. Indeed, to refuse to speak in these ways is to deny Christ before men. And He warns those who do so will be denied before the Father.

What then? Well, the only thing I can say is what I've already been saying for a decade and a half. The Church must recover the courage of her confession. The seminaries must make it a point to teach and talk about such things. Pastors must know and be found willing to proclaim the whole counsel of God, even as the world will call it hate speech, even when the culture will mock, even when members of the flock will most certainly be offended. It's far better to lose security in this life for offending the world than to offend the Shepherd who laid down His life so we would have eternal life (Matt. 16:25).

Something I've said on more than one occasion as a pastor: You cannot love your people if you do not love God more.

Charlie Kirk's death stirs these concerns. Again, this one requires sincere self-reflection. And yet, by holding to Christ in faith, I'm confident it stirs the same forthrightness of the apostles, who said so boldly, "We cannot but speak of what we have seen and heard" (Acts 4:20).

The Last Penny

Three days after Charlie's death came the announcement from Utah's governor. "We got him," were his first words.

I watched the press conference. Admittedly, I thought at first he might start peacocking. But he didn't. Instead, he spoke eloquently, like a man genuinely concerned for the wellbeing of everyone within earshot. He did everything he could to steer the listening country toward reasonableness. He implored all of us to find the off-ramps from the congested political traffic leading to violence and to do so soon.

He made another point about the differences between those who are capable of such navigation and those who are not. His words, while spoken kindly, were stinging. Essentially, he reiterated what our Lord said in Matthew 7. You'll know them by their fruits. One side burns cities to the ground, preferring to call it "mostly peaceful protests." The other holds vigils, only to be called "extremist provocateurs."

The governor was right. He was so very right. Darkness and light are not the same. They're very different. That's the truth. And America was watching, in real time, its stark unveiling. And so, how could anyone be surprised by what happened? When the left spent years tossing around words like "fascist," "Nazi," and "bigot" with reckless abandon, it was only a matter of time before someone came along with a bullet etched with "Hey, fascist! Catch!"

And someone did.

I had another thought while watching the press conference. It may be a little harder to hear. I noticed many thanks were given to all the people in law enforcement, as well as the American citizens who remained vigilant in pursuit of the murderer. This thanks is owed to anyone who devotes his or her life to pursuing evil to restrain it. That said, I wish they offered a tempered thank-you to the killer's father for turning him in, along with a sincere explanation of the depths of the exchange.

Indeed, the Robinson family did what was right, even as the family's reputation was almost certainly poised for obliteration. Had his father not secured him and turned him over, we may still be searching for the killer today. Or perhaps worse, when law enforcement did finally catch up to him, he might have done what cowards in those circumstances often do—commit suicide—leaving the nation struggling for answers, as well as giving a martyr to the demon-like humans supporting him.

There should be no such distractions in a moment like that. Charlie was truth's only real martyr.

I suppose my point is we can at least recognize one act of integrity emerging from within evil's closest circle—a father making a hard decision, choosing truth over blood. Let that be a lesson for all of us. Your allegiance to truth must always be stronger than your allegiance to blood.

But now the real question looms. Justice. What happens next? It is not enough to catch a monster. Society must also reckon with what the monster has done. There can be mercy for a sinner who repents, and yet, God has established boundaries to restrain wickedness and punish evil.

Our Lord spoke to this very tension in Matthew 5:25–26: "Come to terms quickly with your accuser while you are going with him to court, lest your accuser hand you over to the judge, and the judge to the guard, and you be put in prison. Truly, I say to you, you will never get out until you have paid the last penny." Christ's words make it clear: Reconciliation is best. Sort out your differences before needing to employ the law. Because if you don't, judgment will come. And that judgment is not deferred until eternity—it happens here, in this life, at the hands of lawful authority.

This is not to say the killer could not be forgiven. He could. The cross of Christ is broad enough to cover even his sins, should he repent in faith. But forgiveness does not erase earthly consequences. The Lord insists crimes have a cost to be paid, and in this life the offender, forgiven or not, will pay every last penny.

Sometimes, the last penny is the hardest.

So, again, the question: What now? Now, justice runs its full course. In Utah, the killer's life, by his own hand, was forfeited. And if justice means anything, it means the one who murdered must face death himself. The sword was entrusted to the state for precisely such a purpose (Romans 13).

I thank God he was caught. I've prayed for his soul ever since. But I also pray, for the sake of the victims, the community, and the moral fabric of society, that justice would be allowed to run its course. Anything else would be far from mercy—but rather, cruelty in disguise. For Charlie's family, for our nation, and for the sake of truth, justice is required. And if the sword is finally measured against this evil and its legacy, let it be a warning to the children of darkness, and a comfort to the children of light.

Onward!

Like so many across this nation, I can say I knew Charlie and called him my friend. I want to share with you the last text he sent me. He ended the brief back-and-forth with a happy, "Our best days are ahead! Onward!"

To this day, those words echo within my frame with a force I cannot shake.

In the most tremendous sense, for Charlie, those best days are now. His race is finished. His fight is won. He has come into the nearest presence of Christ in heaven, where the crown of righteousness is laid upon his head by the Lord. His best days are not ahead in this world but are right now in the world without end.

So then, to whom is the lingering directive "Onward" now addressed? It is not for Charlie. Not anymore. He has reached the goal. It is, therefore, to us. To you. To me. To the Church still laboring in the shadowed fields of this world. It is a word pressed into the souls of those who remain: Do not falter. Do not retreat. Do not let grief harden into silence. The command is clear. Onward! Charlie's voice is now at rest in the quiet of eternal life. Ours must now grow confidently louder. His steps are stilled in this life. Ours must move even more steadily and faster. His courage has been poured out. Ours must now be filled to the brim.

Charlie's legacy is not a eulogy that fades when everyone goes home. It is a summons.

Consider Paul's words in 2 Timothy 4:7: "I have fought the good fight, I have finished the race, I have kept the faith." Charlie did that. Even so, the fight remains. The race continues. The faith must still be kept. That means the responsibility falls to us—the ones still breathing, still standing, still given the gift of time in this moment of history.

Charlie did not waste his time. He gave it to students, to families, to the Church, to this nation. He stood where others would not. He said what others feared to say. He bore the insults, the smears, the attempted cancellations, and finally, he took a bullet meant to terrify the rest of us into passive quietism.

But read the following carefully.

Silence is not an option. Not for you. Not for me. Not for anyone who dares to call Christ Lord in this fading republic.

So, what now? Do we mourn? Yes, and rightly so. But mourning is not the end. Mourning must stir resolve. Indeed, if Charlie could take his stand on hostile campuses, then surely we can take ours in pulpits, in workplaces, in classrooms, in school board meetings, in conversations with family and friends, in the public square—wherever truth is denied and darkness boasts the upper hand.

I am not describing some sort of advanced-level Christianity for the few brave souls ready to engage. This is simply what it means to be a Christian in an age drunk on lies. You are salt. You are light. You are witnesses. To bury those callings under fear or convenience is to spit on Charlie's grave and, worse, to deny Jesus Christ, the One who lived, suffered, died, and rose again for you.

Of course, there's no use in hiding what any of this really means. It will cost you. You will lose friends. You may lose your job. You may even lose your life. But the greater cost is cowardice. Cowardice is the corrosion of the soul. It is the slow rot of a nation that once knew what it meant to stand when standing was required. Cowardice is precisely what the enemies of truth are counting on in this hour. If fear can muzzle us, if the comfort of safety and security can buy us off, then evil has already won without firing another shot.

But not here. Not now. Not ever.

Charlie's race is finished. Yours is not. His voice is silenced. Yours is not. His courage has been spent. Yours is being summoned. Do not look away. Do not retreat. Do not stand aside waiting for someone else to do what needs to be done. That someone else is you.

For Charlie's heartbroken wife and children, for the Church in desperate need of those who'd engage faithfully, for the country we all love, and above all, for the Lord who gave us breath—get in the game. Pick up the torch. Carry it high. Do not let the darkness have the last word.

I cannot end without saying: To anyone caught in hatred's grip, know this—it is not too late. You can turn. You can be changed. Even for those who would rather raise a fist in rage than extend a hand in kindness, who would rather destroy than build up, who would instead choose death over life—there is still time. The same grace that steadied Charlie's steps is there to steady yours.

Do not surrender your soul to darkness. Lay down your hate. Walk away from the destiny in ruin it promises. Come and stand in a place where light exposes every falsehood and only truth remains.

And then lift your eyes, because it is then you will see—indeed, our best days are ahead!

Onward!

A Glossary of Terms

To navigate the conversation concerned with fostering better engagement in the public square, readers must have certain words or phrases well in hand. The following definitions will aid in this grasping.

Accommodationism. A cooperative view of Church and State, which understands both spheres as distinct and yet interdependent. McCormick Professor of Jurisprudence Emeritus at Princeton University, Alphaeus Mason, described accommodationism as "government acknowledgment of and sometimes support for religion."[1]

Andragogy A term used to describe adult educational processes. First used by Alexander Kapp in 1833 to enunciate Plato's educational framework, researcher Malcolm Knowles later standardized it to mean all forms of adult education.[2]

Cancel culture or *Cancellation.* A societal phenomenon in which a person or group aligns resources against an opponent in order to publicly shame in ways resulting in permanent damage to the opponent's reputation, livelihood, and the like.[3]

Church and State. A general phrase relative to the Establishment Clause of the First Amendment. It refers to the relationship between religious entities and civil authorities.[4]

Classical conditioning. The process of pairing a neutral stimulus with an unconditional stimulus to induce a natural response.[5] A definitive example of this is Ivan Pavlov's experiment in which he rang a bell before feeding a dog. In short, the dog eventually began salivating every time the bell was rung, even without feeding.

Cognitive dissonance. The uneasiness a person experiences when he becomes aware his beliefs and behaviors are misaligned.[6] Leon Festinger first proposed the concept in his book *A Theory of Cognitive Dissonance.*[7]

Constitutionalism. A general term used to describe a system of governance ruled by an established set of "highest" laws that configure and define the government's responsibilities and powers.[8] It should be noted, any given collective's possession of a constitution does not make it constitutionalist. Dictatorships often have constitutions. However, the dictator holds the highest seat of authority rather than the established rule of law.

Critical Race Theory. Richard Delgado and Jean Stefancic define Critical Race Theory and its movement as "a collection of activists and scholars engaged in studying and transforming the relationship among race, racism, and power." They continue:

> The movement considers many of the same issues that conventional civil rights and ethnic studies discourses take up but places them in a broader perspective that includes economics, history, setting, group and self-interest, and emotions and the unconscious. Unlike traditional civil rights discourse, which stresses incrementalism and step-by-step progress, critical race theory questions the very foundations of the liberal order, including equality theory, legal reasoning, Enlightenment rationalism, and neutral principles of constitutional law.[9]

Culture. Often used in a general way to describe accepted societal beliefs and practices influencing the individual. A more precise (and thorough) definition was iterated by Alfred Kroeber and Clyde Kluckhohn in 1952. They wrote:

> Culture consists of patterns, explicit and implicit, of and for behavior acquired and transmitted by symbols, constituting the distinctive achievement of human groups, including their embodiments in artifacts; the essential core of culture consists of traditional (i.e., historically derived and selected) ideas and especially their attached values; culture systems may, on the one hand, be considered as products of action, on the other as conditioning influences upon further action.[10]

Deism. A religious system that believes God established the universe as a self-preserving machine and, after creation, largely withdrew from it. Deism believes God does not engage through supernatural means, preferring instead to engage through natural law.[11]

Disagreement fatigue. A condition born from continued subjection to conflict, resulting in a tired willingness to agree to anything to avoid contentious disagreement.[12]

Dominionism. A political ideology that believes only Christians are qualified to serve in governing roles in society, and once they do, Christ will return.[13]

Establishment Clause. The following phrase within the First Amendment to the United States Constitution: "Congress shall pass no law respecting an establishment of religion." The clause affirms that the legislative branch of the federal government cannot establish an official religion.[14]

Free Exercise Clause. The following phrase immediately following the Establishment Clause within the First Amendment to the United States Constitution: "or prohibiting the free exercise thereof." Akin to the Establishment Clause, the Free Exercise Clause affirms that as the government may not establish an official religion, it may not prohibit an individual citizen's right to practice (believe and act) according to the tenets of a particular faith.[15]

Homiletics. The preparation and practice of a species of public oration typically in service to religious assemblies. Written and preached sermons (or homilies) are the typical fruits of homiletics.[16]

Johnson Amendment. An addition to the Internal Revenue Code adopted in 1954 prohibiting tax-exempt organizations from participating in political campaigns.[17] Concerning the Amendment, a summary seems necessary. This thesis's author commends an explanation he previously wrote and shared on social media in 2020. It reads:

> Firstly, the Amendment states that a non-profit religious organization may not endorse or oppose a particular candidate in a way that results in the imposition of punitive action against members of the organization who endorse or oppose a different candidate, contribute to or use a church's resources for the benefit of one candidate over another. This typically happens when one particular candidate or party is granted open access to a church's membership roster. Secondly, a non-profit religious organization may perform such activities as register their members as voters, distribute non-partisan voting guides, invite candidates to speak, directly address issues and legislation (abortion, marriage, and the like), and even employ the church's resources to move for or against these issues. Preaching is not excluded. Thirdly, as an individual, the pastor or religious leader of a non-profit religious organization may do whatever he or she feels led to do within his or her station—which includes but is not limited to publicly endorsing a candidate, supporting (or encouraging support toward) a party or campaign, and the like, as long as the efforts are not done using the church's material resources. There are no limitations on the

pastors as individuals serving in their offices. The few limitations above that do exist are only for the religious entity as a whole and only if the religious entity is a non-profit organization.[18]

Natural Law. A concept first established in Stoicism to define the unchanging laws of nature. Over time, it has gained the legal connotation of "natural justice." Relative to many Christian denominations, it is understood as the post-fall remnant knowledge of God visible in and through nature.[19] For example, it can be known by the revealed knowledge of God in the Bible that He made humans either male or female. Natural law reveals this not only through biological gender but also by the functions and necessities relative to each. This is to say a child cannot be created without the coupling of both genders' functions.

Pedagogy. A field of study relative to instruction. Specifically, pedagogy includes the science and methodology of imputing knowledge to developing children.[20]

Public square. A term used to define publicly accessible locations and means for ideological presentation and conversation. Typically, the public square refers to government bodies, mass media, and the like.[21]

Radical individualism. The extreme premise supposing individuals are free to do, say, be, and act as they desire apart from communal contexts and without consequence.[22] In short, the individual is most important. Radical individualism stands in contrast to general individualism, which understands even as every individual has inherent rights, he or she remains obligated to the welfare of the community.[23]

Secularism. A term often considered synonymous with "separation of Church and State." In a formal sense, the term is more precisely dissected into three subcategories relative to the aforementioned phrase. The first is the absolute division between religious and state institutions. In other words, a secularist society's government must not allow religion to influence its structure. The second is the freedom of conscience maintained by the rule of law. The third is equal treatment for all amid the absence of discriminatory practices for any reason.[24]

Separationism. The fundamental opposite of accommodationism. Separationism is the absolute division between religion and government, with neither being allowed to cooperate with or accommodate the other.[25]

Two Kingdoms Doctrine. A theological interpretation of Church and State. In an elementary sense, the Two Kingdoms doctrine refers to the absolute rule of Christ exercised in unique ways in two distinct spheres. The kingdom of the left is the civil government's sphere, while the kingdom of the right is the Church's sphere.[26]

Woke. A slang term used to mean one's awareness of past and present social injustice, inequality, and inherent system inequities. In other words, it means "one is 'awake' to the true nature of the world when so many are asleep."[27]

World. A term often used in the New Testament to mean secular culture. This handling emerges from its biblical usage, which refers to sinful creation and its inhabitants' inherent hostility to God.[28] Examples of such usage occur in texts like Hebrews 11:38 and 1 John 3:1. Jesus uses the term in this way in John 14:17, 15:18–19, and 16:8–9.

Endnotes

Introduction

1. Robert O. Paxton, *The Anatomy of Fascism* (Knopf, 2004), 5–8, 218–22.

2. Alan Bullock, *Hitler: A Study in Tyranny* (Harper Perennial, 1991), 389–92; H. R. Trevor-Roper, ed., *Hitler's Table Talk, 1941–1944* (Enigma Books, 2000), entries from July 11 and October 14, 1941; Richard J. Evans, *The Third Reich in Power, 1933–1939* (Penguin, 2006), 224–27.

3. Denis Mack Smith, *Mussolini: A Biography* (Vintage Books, 1983), 15–20.

4. Emilio Gentile, *Politics as Religion* (Princeton University Press, 2006), 59–72; Dinesh D'Souza, *The Big Lie: Exposing the Nazi Roots of the American Left* (Regnery Publishing, 2017), chap. 2; Samuel Gregg, *Reason, Faith, and the Struggle for Western Civilization* (Regnery Gateway, 2019), 165–68.

5. Victoria Barnett, *For the Soul of the People: Protestant Protest Against Hitler* (Oxford University Press, 1992), 1–5; Robert P. Ericksen and Susannah Heschel, eds., *Betrayal: German Churches and the Holocaust* (Fortress Press, 1999), 22–28.

6. Eric Metaxas, *Bonhoeffer: Pastor, Martyr, Prophet, Spy* (Thomas Nelson, 2010), 423–31.

7. Stanley G. Payne, *A History of Fascism, 1914–1945* (University of Wisconsin Press, 1995), 14.

8. Peter Overby, "IRS Apologizes for Aggressive Scrutiny of Conservative Groups," *NPR*, October 27, 2017, sec. Politics, https://www.npr.org/2017/10/27/560308997/irs-apologizes-for-aggressive-scrutiny-of-conservative-groups.

9. Victor Nava and Bruce Golding, "Suppression of Right-Wing Users Exposed in Latest 'Twitter Files,'" *New York Post*, December 8, 2022, https://nypost.com/2022/12/08/suppression-of-right-wing-users-exposed-in-latest-twitter-files/.

10. Erin Elmore, "PayPal, Venmo Targets Conservative Accounts," Turning Point USA, September 23, 2022, https://www.tpusa.com/live/paypal-venmo-target-conservative-accounts.

11. "Free Speech: The Biden Administration's Chilling of Parents' Fundamental Rights," legislation, accessed May 22, 2025, https://www.congress.gov/event/118th-congress/house-event/115531/text.

12. "AG Paxton Sues Biden Administration for Silencing Parents, Labeling Them 'Terrorists' | Office of the Attorney General," accessed May 22, 2025, https://www.texasattorneygeneral.gov/news/releases/ag-paxton-sues-biden-administration-silencing-parents-labeling-them-terrorists.

Chapter 1

1. Paula Schlueter Ross, "Reversing the LCMS Membership Decline: Not Just by Having More Children," Reporter, February 28, 2017, https://reporter.lcms.org/2017/reversing-lcms-membership-decline/.

2. https://www.pewresearch.org/short-reads/2018/01/22/american-religious-groups-vary-widely-in-their-views-of-abortion/

3. Steve Bruce, *God Is Dead: Secularization in the West* (Wiley-Blackwell, 2002), 13.

4. Saul K. Padover, ed., *The Complete Jefferson* (Duell, Sloan & Pearce, Inc., 1943), 120.

5. Padover, 958.

6. Lindsay F. Wiley, "Extreme Religious Liberty Is Undermining Public Health," *New York Times*, September 15, 2022, sec. Opinion, https://www.nytimes.com/2022/09/15/opinion/religious-liberty-public-health.html.

7. "Why America's 'Nones' Don't Identify with a Religion," Pew Research Center, August 8, 2018, https://www.pewresearch.org/fact-tank/2018/08/08/why-americas-nones-dont-identify-with-a-religion/.

8. Adam MacInnis, "26 Million Americans Stopped Reading the Bible Regularly During COVID-19," *Christianity Today*, April 20, 2022, https://www.christianitytoday.com/news/2022/april/state-of-bible-reading-decline-report-26-million.html.

Chapter 2

1. Daniel Silliman, "Decline of Christianity Shows No Signs of Stopping," *Christianity Today*, September 13, 2022, https://www.christianitytoday.com/news/2022/september/christian-decline-inexorable-nones-rise-pew-study.html.

2. Craig A. Carter, "The Decline of Nicene Orthodoxy: A Monthly Journal of Religion and Public Life," *First Things*, January 2022, 1–7.

3. David Fowler, Jon Musgrave, and Jill Musgrave, "A Traditional Protestant Church Experiencing Substantial Membership Decline: An Organizational Strength Analysis and Observations to Attend or Leave the Institution," *International Journal of Organization Theory and Behavior* 23, no. 3 (2020): 207–23, https://doi.org/10.1108/IJOTB-02-2019-0012.

4. Michael Levitt, "America's Christian Majority Is on Track to End," *NPR*, September 17, 2022, sec. Religion, https://www.npr.org/2022/09/17/1123508069/religion-christianity-muslim-atheist-agnostic-church-lds-pew.

5. David Bradshaw and Frederica Mathewes-Green, *Healing Humanity: Confronting Our Moral Crisis*, ed. David C. Ford, Alfred Kentigern Siewers, and Alexander F. C. Webster (Holy Trinity Seminary Press, 2020), 132. Chad Hatfield affirms, "The 'taming' of religion has now become an attack from the inside. The drift and decline of mainline Protestantism is, of course, well documented."

6. Reem Nadeem, "Modeling the Future of Religion in America," *Pew Research Center's Religion & Public Life Project* (blog), September 13, 2022, https://www.pewresearch.org/religion/2022/09/13/modeling-the-future-of-religion-in-america/.

7. Consider such volumes as Aubrey Malphurs's *Advanced Strategic Planning: A 21st Century Model for Church and Ministry Leaders* (BakerBooks, 2013), Peter Greer's and Chris Horst's *Mission Drift: The Unspoken Crisis Facing Leaders, Charities, and Churches* (Bethany House, 2014), and Tim Suttle's *Shrink: Faithful Ministry in a Church-Growth Culture* (Zondervan, 2014).

8. Malphurs, *Advanced Strategic Planning*, 196. Malphurs's book, a standard for many church leaders, is an exemplary demonstration of corporate methodology superseding traditional pastoral care methods.

9. Oscar Wilde, *The Picture of Dorian Gray* (Bernhard Tauchnitz, 1908), 28.

10. Erwin Chemerinsky, "No, It Is Not a Christian Nation, and It Never Has Been and Should Not Be One," *Roger Williams University Law Review* 26, no. 2. Article 5 (Spring 2021): 406–7.

11. Tiffany E. Piland, "The Influence and Legacy of Deism in Eighteenth-Century America" (Master of Liberal Studies, Rollins College, 2011), 117.

12. J. C. D. Clark, "How Did the American Revolution Relate to the French? Richard Price, the Age of Revolutions, and the Enlightenment," *Modern Intellectual History* 19, no. 1 (2022): 118–19, https://doi.org/10.1017/S1479244320000372.

13. Clark, 116–17, 120, 123.

14. Angus J. L. Menuge, *Christ and Culture in Dialogue: Constructive Themes and Practical Applications*, ed. William R. Cario, Alberto L. Garcia, and Dale E. Griffin (Concordia Publishing House, 1999), 191.

15. David L. Holmes, *The Faiths of the Founding Fathers* (Oxford University Press, 2006), 163–64.

16. Steven D. Smith, *Christians and Pagans in the City: Culture Wars from the Tiber to the Potomac* (William B. Eerdmans Publishing Company, 2018), 295–96.

17. Geoffrey R. Stone, "The World of the Framers: A Christian Nation?," *University of California Law Review* 56 (October 2008): 7–8.

18. Christopher Grasso, *Skepticism and American Faith: From the Revolution to the Civil War* (Oxford University Press, 2018), 72, 84, 124, 155, 326.

19. Paul F. Boller, *George Washington & Religion* (Southern Methodist University Press, 1963), 89–90, 100.

20. Shun-hing Chan, "The Political Influence of Mainline Protestant Churches in Hong Kong," *China Review* 21, no. 4 (2021): 229.

21. Gary DeMar, *America's Christian History: The Untold Story* (American Vision, 2005), 51.

22. William J. Federer, *America's God and Country: Encyclopedia of Quotations* (Amerisearch, Inc., 1994), 456.

23. Alexis de Tocqueville, *Democracy in America: Volume I* (Scratcherd and Adams, 1839), 303.

24. Samuel Adams, *Samuel Adams, Volume III: Life & Public Services of Samuel Adams*, ed. William V. Wells (Little, Brown & Co., 1865), 379.

25. Mark David Hall, "Did America Have a Christian Founding?," The Heritage Foundation, June 7, 2011, https://www.heritage.org/political-process/report/did-america-have-christian-founding.

26. Eric Metaxas, *Letter to the American Church* (Salem Books, 2022), x.

27. "Oregon Secretary of State Administrative Rules," accessed May 27, 2025, https://secure.sos.state.or.us/oard/viewSingleRule.action?ruleVrsnRsn=309115.

28. Dale E. Soden, "Jason Lee (1803–1845)," Oregon Encyclopedia, accessed May 27, 2025, https://www.oregonencyclopedia.org/articles/lee_jason/.

29. James Hutchinson Smylie, "American Clergymen and the Constitution of the United States of America" (Princeton Theological Seminary, 1958).

30. John Eidsmoe and D. James Kennedy, *Christianity and the Constitution: The Faith of Our Founding Fathers* (Baker Academic, 1995).

31. Michael Cecere, "The Fighting Parson's Farewell Sermon," *Journal of the American Revolution* (blog), April 15, 2020, https://allthingsliberty.com/2020/04/the-fighting-parsons-farewell-sermon/.

32. Dale Carpenter, "VIEWPOINT: John 'Peter' Muhlenberg—One of Virginia's Finest," October 14, 2023, https://royalexaminer.com/john-peter-muhlenberg-one-of-virginias-finest/.but overcome evil with good" (Romans 12:21

33. "The First Speaker of the House, Frederick A.C. Muhlenberg of Pennsylvania | US House of Representatives: History, Art & Archives," accessed May 27, 2025, https://history.house.gov/Historical-Highlights/1800-1850/The-first-Speaker-of-the-House,-Frederick-A-C--Muhlenberg-of-Pennsylvania/.

Chapter 3

1. Chan, "The Political Influence of Mainline Protestant Churches in Hong Kong," 230.

2. Larry Golemon, "Educating Clergy as Culture-Builders: Can This Long Tradition Be Reclaimed?," *Teaching Theology & Religion* 24, no. 2 (2021): 72, https://doi.org/10.1111/teth.12587.

3. Golemon, "Educating Clergy as Culture-Builders," 77.

4. Metaxas, *Letter to the American Church*, xii–xiii.

5. Metaxas, 2, 5, 9, 85.

6. Todd Starnes, "City of Houston Demands Pastors Turn over Sermons," Fox News, updated May 7, 2015, https://www.foxnews.com/opinion/city-of-houston-demands-pastors-turn-over-sermons.

7. Mike Morris, "Equal Rights Law Opponents Deliver Signatures Seeking Repeal," July 3, 2014, https://www.houstonchronicle.com/news/politics/houston/article/Equal-rights-law-opponents-deliver-signatures-5599272.php?t=63159f4ad9cf61987c#/0.

8. Sarah Pulliam Bailey, "Houston Subpoenas Pastors' Sermons in Gay Rights Ordinance Case," *The Washington Post*, October 15, 2014, https://www.washingtonpost.com/national/religion/houston-subpoenas-pastors-sermons-in-gay-rights-ordinance-case/2014/10/15/9b848ff0-549d-11e4-b86d-184ac281388d_story.html.

Chapter 4

1. Michael A. Conway, "Changing Foundations: Identity, Church and Culture," *The Furrow* 69, no. 2 (2018): 90–91.

2. Conway, 93.

3. Voddie T. Baucham, *Fault Lines: The Social Justice Movement and Evangelicalism's Looming Catastrophe* (Salem Books, 2022), 38.

4. Timothy P. Carney, *Alienated America: Why Some Places Thrive While Others Collapse* (Harper, 2019), 119–20, 287.

5. Robert D. Putnam, *American Grace: How Religion Divides and Unites Us* (Simon & Schuster, 2012).

6. Carney, *Alienated America*, 136.

7. Jeff Myers, *Truth Changes Everything: How People of Faith Can Transform the World in Times of Crisis* (Baker Books, 2022), 57–74.

8. Tobin Grant, "The Great Decline: 60 Years of Religion in One Graph," *Religion News Service* (blog), January 28, 2014, https://religionnews.com/2014/01/27/great-decline-religion-united-states-one-graph/.

9. Gregory A. Smith, *Modeling the Future of Religion in America* (Pew Research Center, 2022), 7, 21.

10. Gregory A. Smith, "In U.S., Far More Support Than Oppose Separation of Church and State" (Pew Research Center, October 28, 2021), 13.

The survey's methodology explanation notes on page 12 that "because [the separationist category] is so large, the 'church-state separationist' category is sometimes divided into two groups in this report."

11. Smith, "In U.S., Far More Support than Oppose Separation of Church and State," 18. The majority ranged "from 58% who say religious displays should be kept off public property to 95% who say the federal government should never declare any official religion."

12. Conway, "Changing Foundations," 93.

13. Conway, 94.

14. George Barna, "American Worldview Inventory 2022: Release #5: Shocking Results Concerning the Worldview of Christian Pastors" (Cultural Research Center, May 10, 2022), 1–2.

15. George Barna, "God's People Want to Know" (American Culture & Faith Institute, August 2015), 11.

16. Barna, 5.

17. Barna, 3.

18. Martin Luther, *Luther's Works*, ed. Jaroslav Jan Pelikan, trans. Martin H. Bertram, vol. 24 (Concordia Publishing House, 1961), 202–6.

19. Wesley Huff, "Netflix's Cuties: A Social Commentary Gone Awry," Wesley Huff, September 24, 2020, https://www.wesleyhuff.com/blog/2020/9/23/cuties.

20. By Jolie McCullough and Stacy Fernández, "Texas Politicians Fueled Criticism of 'Cuties.' Now, Netflix Is Facing Criminal Charges in a Small East Texas County," *The Texas Tribune*, October 6, 2020, https://www.texastribune.org/2020/10/06/texas-tyler-county-netflix-cuties/.

21. Martin Luther and Philip S. Watson, *Luther's Works, Volume 33: Career of the Reformer III* (Fortress Press, 1972), 24.

22. Dietrich Bonhoeffer and Geffrey B. Kelly, *A Testament to Freedom: The Essential Writings of Dietrich Bonhoeffer*, ed. F. Burton Nelson (Harpercollins, 1990), 432.

23. Bonhoeffer and Kelly, 432.

24. *Luther's Works*, Volume 45 (Christian in Society II), ed. Helmut T. Lehmann (Concordia Publishing House, 1962), 352 .

25. *Luther's Works*, 352.

26. Eberhard Bethge, *Dietrich Bonhoeffer: A Biography*, ed. Victoria J. Barnett (Fortress Press, 2000), 483–85.

Chapter 5

1. Matt Walsh, *Church of Cowards: A Wake-Up Call to Complacent Christians* (Regnery Gateway, 2020), 2.

2. Walsh, 3.

3. Walsh, 23–24.

4. Baucham, *Fault Lines*, 2.

5. Natasha Crain, *Faithfully Different: Regaining Biblical Clarity in a Secular Culture* (Harvest House Publishers, 2022), 20–21.

6. Crain, 29.

7. Crain, 91.

8. David Bradshaw and Frederica Mathewes-Green, *Healing Humanity: Confronting Our Moral Crisis*, ed. David C. Ford, Alfred Kentigern Siewers, and Alexander F. C. Webster (Holy Trinity Seminary Press, 2020), 18.

9. Bradshaw and Mathewes-Green, 156.

10. Joshua Steely, "Must Say No," *Touchstone: A Journal of Mere Christianity* (September/October 2019), https://www.touchstonemag.com/archives/article.php?id=32-05-023-v.

11. H. Jack Lang, *The Wit and Wisdom of Abraham Lincoln as Reflected in His Briefer Letters and Speeches* (World Publishing, 1942), 257.

12. John A. O'Brien, "Seeking God's Will: President Lincoln and Rev. Dr. Gurley," *Journal of the Abraham Lincoln Association* 39, no. 2 (Summer 2018), http://hdl.handle.net/2027/spo.2629860.0039.204.

13. "Thurlow Weed (1797–1882)," *Mr. Lincoln and Friends* (blog), accessed May 27, 2025, http://www.mrlincolnandfriends.org/the-journalists/thurlow-weed/.

14. Lang, *The Wit and Wisdom of Abraham Lincoln*, 261.

15. Lang, 261.

16. Abraham Lincoln, *Lincoln: Speeches and Writings (1859–1865)* (Library of America, 1989), 686.

17. Lincoln, 686.

18. Lincoln, 686.

19. Lang, *The Wit and Wisdom of Abraham Lincoln*, 261–62.

Chapter 6

1. Matt Walsh, *Church of Cowards: A Wake-Up Call to Complacent Christians* (Regnery Gateway, 2020), 4–7.

2. Gerhard O. Forde, *On Being a Theologian of the Cross: Reflections on Luther's Heidelberg Disputation, 1518* (Wm. B. Eerdmans Publishing Co., 1997), 12–13.

3. Martin Luther, *Career of the Reformer, I*, ed. J. J. Pelikan, H. C. Oswald, and Helmut T. Lehmann, American Edition, vol. 31, Luther's Works (Fortress Press, 1957), 40.

4. Walsh, *Church of Cowards*, 76, 142.

5. Carl R. Trueman, *The Rise and Triumph of the Modern Self: Cultural Amnesia, Expressive Individualism, and the Road to Sexual Revolution* (Crossway, 2020), 93.

6. Trueman, 383.

7. Trueman, 389.

8. Eric Metaxas, *Letter to the American Church* (Salem Books, 2022), 125–29.

9. Erwin W. Lutzer, *No Reason to Hide: Standing for Christ in a Collapsing Culture* (Harvest House Publishers, 2022), 30.

10. Lutzer, 166, 169.

11. Jo Renee Formicola, "The Catholic Religious Presence in Civil Society: A Waning Influence," *Religions* 12, no. 4 (2021): 260, https://doi.org/10.3390/rel12040248.

12. Formicola, 250.

13. Formicola, 260.

14. Formicola, 254.

15. Larry Golemon, "Educating Clergy as Culture-Builders," *Teaching Theology &* Religion 24, no. 2 (July 26, 2021), 73, https://doi.org/10.1111/teth.12587.

16. Owen Strachan, *Christianity and Wokeness: How the Social Justice Movement Is Hijacking the Gospel—and the Way to Stop It* (Salem Books, 2021), 47–49.

17. Strachan, 50.

18. Mary Eberstadt, *How the West Really Lost God: A New Theory of Secularization* (Templeton Press, 2014), 39.

19. For more, see James Lindsay, *The Marxification of Education: Paulo Freire's Critical Marxism and the Theft of Education* (New Discourses); James Lindsay, "Paulo Freire and the Marxist Transformation of the Church," August 22, 2022, https://newdiscourses.com/2022/08/paulo-freire-and-the-marxist-transformation-of-the-church/.

Chapter 7

1. Matt Walsh, *Church of Cowards: A Wake-Up Call to Complacent Christians* (Regnery Gateway, 2020), 54.

2. Walsh, 111.

3. For clarification, the Church Militant is the worldwide collective of believers on earth, while the Church Triumphant describes the gathered believers in heaven.

4. Walsh, *Church of Cowards*, 154–56.

5. Walsh, 171, 174–75.

6. Michael A. Conway, "Changing Foundations: Identity, Church and Culture," *The Furrow* 69, no. 2 (2018): 91.

7. Conway, 91.

8. David Bradshaw and Frederica Mathewes-Green, *Healing Humanity: Confronting Our Moral Crisis*, ed. David C. Ford, Alfred Kentigern Siewers, and Alexander F. C. Webster (Holy Trinity Seminary Press, 2020), 20.

9. Erwin W. Lutzer, *No Reason to Hide: Standing for Christ in a Collapsing Culture* (Harvest House Publishers, 2022), 261.

10. David P. Scaer, *The Sermon on the Mount: The Church's First Statement of the Gospel* (Concordia Publishing House, 2000), 91.

11. Scaer, 91.

12. Lutzer, *No Reason to Hide*, 211.

13. Kristina Millare/CNA, "EU Watchdog Reports Alarming Rise in Christian Persecution, Calls for Protections," NCR, August 22, 2024, https://www.ncregister.com/cna/eu-watchdog-reports-alarming-rise-in-christian-persecution-calls-for-protections.

14. "World Watch List 2025," accessed May 28, 2025, https://www.opendoors.org/en-US/persecution/countries/.

15. "Scotland's New Hate Crime Law Could Criminalize the Church's Teaching on Sex and Gender," Missouri Catholic Conference, April 25, 2024, https://mocatholic.org/scotlands-new-hate-crime-law-could-criminalize-the-churchs-teaching-on-sex-and-gender/.

16. Julie Zauzmer, "Clergy Gather to Bless One of the Only U.S. Clinics Performing Late-Term Abortions," *The Washington Post*, January 29, 2018, https://www.washingtonpost.com/news/acts-of-faith/wp/2018/01/29/clergy-gather-to-bless-an-abortion-clinic-which-provides-rare-late-term-abortions-in-bethesda/.

17. Caitlin O'Kane, "What Is Prop 3? Voters in Michigan Approve Abortion Rights Amendment," CBS News, November 9, 2022, https://www.cbsnews.com/news/what-is-prop-3-election-2022-michigan-abortion-rights-constitutional-amendment/.

18. Zack Budryk, "Michigan Funeral Home to Pay $250K in Settlement over Transgender Discrimination Case," The Hill, December 2, 2020, https://thehill.com/regulation/court-battles/528360-michigan-funeral-home-to-pay-250000-in-settlement-over-transgender/; John Stonestreet and Jared Hayden, "Jack Phillips Dragged Back to Court - Breakpoint," Breakpoint, July 2, 2024, https://breakpoint.org/jack-phillips-dragged-back-to-court/; Jonathan Oosting, "Judge Slams Dana Nessel in Gay Adoption Case for 'Targeted Attack' on Religion," Bridge Michigan, September 26, 2019, https://www.bridgemi.com/michigan-government/judge-slams-dana-nessel-gay-adoption-case-targeted-attack-religion.

19. Ryan Foley and Christian Post Reporter, "Biden Is a 'Cafeteria Catholic,' Cardinal Says in Rebuke," June 19, 2024, https://www.christianpost.com/news/cardinal-sarah-says-biden-is-a-cafeteria-catholic.html; Daniel Payne/CNA, "Cardinal Gregory: Biden 'Picks and Chooses' Parts of Catholic Faith," NCR, April 1, 2024, https://www.ncregister.com/cna/cardinal-gregory-biden-picks-and-chooses-parts-of-catholic-faith.

20. Carmyn Gutierrez, "Trailer Filled with Bibles 'Intentionally' Set on Fire Near Church Easter Sunday in Tennessee," ABC7 Chicago, April 1, 2024, https://abc7chicago.com/easter-sunday-bibles-burn-trailer-set-on-fire-mt-juliet/14599128/.

21. John Blaydes, *The Educator's Book of Quotes* (Corwin Press, 2003), 131.

Chapter 8

1. Stanley Hauerwas and William H. Willimon, *Resident Aliens: Life in the Christian Colony* (Abingdon Press, 1989), 43.

2. Hauerwas and Willimon, 24–25.

3. Stanley Hauerwas, *A Cross-Shattered Church: Reclaiming the Theological Heart of Preaching* (Brazos Press, 2009), 148.

4. Hauerwas, 148.

5. William H. Willimon, *Peculiar Speech: Preaching to the Baptized* (William B. Eerdmans, 1992), 53.

6. Timothy P. Carney, *Alienated America: Why Some Places Thrive While Others Collapse* (Harper, 2019), 90.

7. Carney, 116.

8. Carney, 256.

9. Carney, 248, 254–55, 298–99.

10. Carl R. Trueman, *The Rise and Triumph of the Modern Self: Cultural Amnesia, Expressive Individualism, and the Road to Sexual Revolution* (Crossway, 2020), 404.

11. Here, pluralism means diverse views within a singular context or community.

12. J. Hector St. John de Crevecouer, *Letters from an American Farmer*, ed. Susan Manning (Oxford University Press, 1997), 45–46, 48–51.

13. David Bradshaw and Frederica Mathewes-Green, *Healing Humanity: Confronting Our Moral Crisis*, ed. David C. Ford, Alfred Kentigern Siewers, and Alexander F. C. Webster (Holy Trinity Seminary Press, 2020), 96.

14. Bradshaw and Mathewes-Green, 39.

15. Bradshaw and Mathewes-Green, 27.

16. Natasha Crain, *Faithfully Different: Regaining Biblical Clarity in a Secular Culture* (Harvest House Publishers, 2022), 52, 55.

17. David Seckler, *Thorstein Veblen and the Institutionalists: A Study in the Social Philosophy of Economics* (Colorado Associated University Press, 1975), 79.

18. Paul D. Bush, "'Radical Individualism' vs. Institutionalism, II: Philosophical Dualisms as Apologetic Constructs Based on Obsolete Psychological Preconceptions," *The American Journal of Economics and Sociology* 40, no. 3 (1981): 288.

19. Trueman, *The Rise and Triumph of the Modern Self*, 35.

20. Roderick T. Long, "The Classical Roots of Radical Individualism," *Social Philosophy and Policy* 24, no. 2 (2007): 278, https://doi.org/10.1017/S0265052507070252.

21. Trueman, *The Rise and Triumph of the Modern Self*, 39–40.

22. Bradshaw and Mathewes-Green, *Healing Humanity*, 19.

23. Michael Mascolo, "Is Radical Individualism Destroying Our Moral Compass?" *Psychology Today*, December 11, 2016, https://www.psychology today.com/us/blog/values-matter/201612/is-radical-individualism-destroy ing-our-moral-compass. Also see Jonathan Haidt, "Morality," *Perspectives on Psychological Science* 3, no. 1 (January 1, 2008): 65–72.

24. Daniel A. Cox, "Generation Z and the Future of Faith in America," *The Survey Center on American Life* (blog), March 24, 2022, https://www .americansurveycenter.org/research/generation-z-future-of-faith/.

25. Carney, *Alienated America*, 192–93.

26. Carney, 181.

27. Carney, 183.

28. Carney, 183.

29. Michael A. Conway, "Changing Foundations: Identity, Church and Culture," *The Furrow* 69, no. 2 (2018): 94.

30. Conway, 97.

31. Jeff Myers, *Truth Changes Everything: How People of Faith Can Transform the World in Times of Crisis* (Baker Books, 2022), 29.

32. Myers, 35–38.

33. Myers, 41.

34. Myers, 42–48.

35. Lia Eustachewich, "Man Loves His MacBook So Much, He Decided to Marry It," *New York Post*, September 7, 2017, https://nypost.com/2017/09/07/man-loves-his-macbook-so-much-he-decided-to-marry-it/.

36. Deborah Hastings, "Dutch Woman Will Marry Dog After Her Husband—a Cat—Dies," *New York Daily News*, July 21, 2015, https://www.ny dailynews.com/2015/07/21/dutch-woman-will-marry-dog-after-her-hus band-a-cat-dies/; "MarryYourPet - The Pet and People Wedding Specialists," accessed May 28, 2025, http://marryyourpet.com/; Bob Unruh, "Court Told: Humans Could Marry Animals," WorldNetDaily, November 10, 2014, https://www.wnd.com/2014/11/court-told-humans-could-marry-animals/.

37. Emma Stein, "Girls Are in at Boy Scouts of America: How It's Going After 3 Years," June 6, 2022, https://www.freep.com/story/news/local/michigan/2022/06/06/coed-girl-boy-scouts-of-america-michigan /9894220002/.

38. Emily James, "Canadian Man Leaves Family to Be Transgender Six-Year-Old Girl," *Daily Mail*, December 11, 2015, https://www.daily mail.co.uk/femail/article-3356084/I-ve-gone-child-Husband-father-seven

-52-leaves-wife-kids-live-transgender-SIX-YEAR-OLD-girl-named-Stefonknee.html; Candace Amos, “Transgender Woman Leaves Wife and 7 Kids to Live as a 6-Year-Old Girl,” *New York Daily News*, December 12, 2015, https://www.nydailynews.com/2015/12/12/transgender-woman-leaves-wife-and-7-kids-to-live-as-a-6-year-old-girl/.

39. “Reports of Committees of the House of Representatives Made During the First Session of the Thirty-Third Congress,” n.d., 6.

40. J. J. Boudinot, ed., *The Life, Public Services, Addresses, and Letters of Elias Boudinot: Volume I* (Houghton, Mifflin & Co., 1896), 19–21.

41. Jedidiah Morse, “A Sermon: Exhibiting the Present Dangers and Consequent Duties of the Citizens of the United States of America, Delivered at Charlestown, April 25” (Samuel Etheridge, 1799), 9.

42. “Obama's 2006 Speech on Faith and Politics,” *The New York Times*, June 28, 2006, https://www.nytimes.com/2006/06/28/us/politics/2006obamaspeech.html.

Chapter 9

1. Eric Metaxas, *Letter to the American Church* (Salem Books, 2022), 8, 11.

2. Metaxas, 19, 65, 95–105.

3. Metaxas, 53.

4. Metaxas, 42.

5. Carl R. Trueman, *The Rise and Triumph of the Modern Self: Cultural Amnesia, Expressive Individualism, and the Road to Sexual Revolution* (Crossway, 2020), 399.

6. Michael A. Conway, “Changing Foundations: Identity, Church and Culture,” *The Furrow* 69, no. 2 (2018): 93.

7. Timothy P. Carney, *Alienated America: Why Some Places Thrive While Others Collapse* (Harper, 2019), 287.

8. “Pastors Share Confidence, Struggles & Concerns Around Preaching,” Barna Group, June 8, 2022, https://www.barna.com/research/preaching-confidence/.

9. “Pastors Share Top Reasons They've Considered Quitting Ministry in the Past Year,” Barna Group, April 27, 2022, https://www.barna.com/research/pastors-quitting-ministry/.

10. Patrick Svitek, “Beto O'Rourke Targets Tax-Exempt Status for Religious Institutions Opposing Gay Marriage,” *The Texas Tribune*, October 11, 2019, https://www.texastribune.org/2019/10/11/beto-orourke-religious-institutions-gay-marriage/.

11. Jacob Bronowski, *The Ascent of Man* (Random House, 2011), 92–93.

12. William Shakespeare, *Coriolanus*, ed. Peter Holland (Bloomsbury Publishing, 2013), 3.2.76.

13. William Hazlitt, *Men and Manners: Sketches and Essays* (Illustrated London Library, 1852), 97.

14. Hazlitt, 99.

Chapter 10

1. Michael A. Conway, "Changing Foundations: Identity, Church and Culture," *The Furrow* 69, no. 2 (2018): 94.

2. Conway, "Changing Foundations," 94.

3. Paola Pascual-Ferrá, "The Measurement of Trust in Communication Research," *Communication Research Trends* 39, no. 4 (2020): 17.

4. Jeff Myers, *Truth Changes Everything: How People of Faith Can Transform the World in Times of Crisis* (Baker Books, 2022), 54–55.

5. Myers, 197.

6. Myers, 197.

7. Heather J. Sharkey and Jeffrey Edward Green, eds., *The Changing Terrain of Religious Freedom* (University of Pennsylvania Press, 2021), 37–39.

8. Erwin W. Lutzer, *No Reason to Hide: Standing for Christ in a Collapsing Culture* (Harvest House Publishers, 2022), 52.

9. Lutzer, 153.

10. Eric Metaxas, *Letter to the American Church* (Salem Books, 2022), 88.

11. Natasha Crain, *Faithfully Different: Regaining Biblical Clarity in a Secular Culture* (Harvest House Publishers, 2022), 115–18.

12. Crain, 32.

13. Voddie T. Baucham, *Fault Lines: The Social Justice Movement and Evangelicalism's Looming Catastrophe* (Salem Books, 2022) 8, 22, 28.

14. "Definition of Woke," accessed February 18, 2023, https://www.merriam-webster.com/dictionary/woke.

15. Owen Strachan, *Christianity and Wokeness: How the Social Justice Movement Is Hijacking the Gospel—and the Way to Stop It* (Salem Books, 2021), 59, 66–70, 73, 79, 105.

16. Adam S. Francisco, "Awake or Woke: The Outline of a Lutheran View," *Lutheran Witness*, April 2023, 22.

17. Crain, *Faithfully Different*, 19–20.

18. Dietrich Bonhoeffer, *Letters & Papers from Prison*, ed. Eberhard Bethge (Collier Books, 1972), 135.

19. Bonhoeffer, 135.

20. Bonhoeffer, 136.

21. Bonhoeffer, 137.

22. Bonhoeffer, 137.

23. Bonhoeffer, 137.

24. Bonhoeffer, 138.

25. Bonhoeffer, 138.

Chapter 11

1. Theodore G. Tappert, ed., *The Book of Concord: The Confessions of the Evangelical Lutheran Church* (Fortress Press, 1959), 37–38.

2. Erwin W. Lutzer, *No Reason to Hide: Standing for Christ in a Collapsing Culture* (Harvest House Publishers, 2022), 33.

3. Tappert, *The Book of Concord*, 81–94. For a slightly more thorough but still relatively succinct explanation, please see Christopher I. Thoma, "Two Kingdoms: Is There a Line between Christ and Caesar?," *The Lutheran Witness*, January 2015, 18–19.

4. Eric Metaxas, *Letter to the American Church* (Salem Books, 2022), 9.

5. G. R. Elton, *The New Cambridge Modern History: Volume 2, The Reformation, 1520-1559* (Cambridge University Press, 1990), 191.

6. Matthew Colvin, trans., *The Magdeburg Confession: 13th of April 1550 A.D.* (Matthew Trewhella, 2012), 6.

7. Colvin, 7.

8. Colvin, 7.

9. Colvin, 67.

10. Eric Metaxas, *Bonhoeffer: Pastor, Martyr, Prophet, Spy* (Thomas Nelson, 2010), 281.

11. Theodore Graebner, "Christian Citizenship: An Essay," Convention of the English District, Evangelical Lutheran Synod of Missouri, Ohio, and Other States (Concordia Publishing House, 1937), 5.

12. Metaxas, *Bonhoeffer*, 360–61.

13. Metaxas, 153.

14. Samuel Deressa, "Luther on Two Kingdoms Theology and Christian Education," *Lutheran Theological Journal* 55, no. 3 (December 2021): 155.

15. Deressa, 156.

16. Colvin, *The Magdeburg Confession: 13th of April 1550 A.D.*, 54, 59, 63–65, 71, 79–80, 83.

17. Volker Leppin, "The Scope and Limits of Secular Authority: On the Origins and Context of Luther's Doctrine of the Two Kingdoms," *Lutheran Theological Journal* 48, no. 2 (August 2014): 91.

18. Leppin, 97.

19. Franky Schaeffer, *A Time for Anger: The Myth of Neutrality* (Crossway Books, 1984), 62.

20. Mark Storslee, "Church Taxes and the Original Understanding of the Establishment Clause," *University of Pennsylvania Law Review*, December 2020, 127, Gale Business: Insights.

21. "The Constitution of the United States," National Archives, October 30, 2015, https://www.archives.gov/founding-docs/constitution.

22. Tom Ginsburg, Zachary Elkins, and James Melton, *The Endurance of National Constitutions* (Cambridge University Press, 2009).

23. "Page d'accueil | Conseil constitutionnel," accessed May 16, 2025, https://www.conseil-constitutionnel.fr/landing/21.

24. John R. Vile, *Founding Documents of America: Documents Decoded* (Bloomsbury Publishing USA, 2015), 315.

25. Max Farrand, ed., *The Records of the Federal Convention of 1787, Volume 3* (Yale University Press, 1911), 87.

Chapter 12

1. C. S. Lewis, *The Great Divorce* (Touchstone, 1996), 10.

2. See content above in chapter 7: "[The church] does not shrink from engagement but understands humility and love as truth's best vehicle."

3. Owen Strachan, *Christianity and Wokeness: How the Social Justice Movement Is Hijacking the Gospel—and the Way to Stop It* (Salem Books, 2021), 50.

4. Robert C. Solomon, *The Joy of Philosophy: Thinking Thin Versus the Passionate Life* (Oxford University Press, 2003), 200.

5. Strachan, *Christianity and Wokeness*, 53.

6. David Bradshaw and Frederica Mathewes-Green, *Healing Humanity: Confronting Our Moral Crisis*, ed. David C. Ford, Alfred Kentigern Siewers, and Alexander F. C. Webster (Holy Trinity Seminary Press, 2020), 44.

7. Natasha Crain, *Faithfully Different: Regaining Biblical Clarity in a Secular Culture* (Harvest House Publishers, 2022), 22.

8. Eric Metaxas, *Bonhoeffer: Pastor, Martyr, Prophet, Spy* (Thomas Nelson, 2010), 447.

9. Erwin W. Lutzer, *No Reason to Hide: Standing for Christ in a Collapsing Culture* (Harvest House Publishers, 2022), 18.

10. Lutzer, 20.

11. Lutzer, 84–85.

12. Lutzer, 85.

13. Lutzer, 231.

14. Lutzer, 207.

15. Eric Metaxas, *Letter to the American Church* (Salem Books, 2022), 84.

16. Michael Conway, "Changing Foundations: Identity, Church and Culture," *The Furrow* 69, no. 2 (2018): 91.

17. Carl R. Trueman, *The Rise and Triumph of the Modern Self: Cultural Amnesia, Expressive Individualism, and the Road to Sexual Revolution* (Crossway, 2020), 54–55.

18. Trueman, 76–77.

19. Richard John Neuhaus, *The Naked Public Square: Religion and Democracy in America* (Wm. B. Eerdmans Publishing, 1986).1986

20. Larry Golemon, "Educating Clergy as Culture-Builders: Can This Long Tradition Be Reclaimed?," *Teaching Theology & Religion* 24, no. 2 (2021): 77.

21. Jo Renee Formicola, "The Catholic Religious Presence in Civil Society: A Waning Influence," *Religions* 12, no. 4 (2021): 250.

22. W. Bradford Littlejohn, *The Two Kingdoms: A Guide for the Perplexed* (The Davenant Press, 2017), 51–52.

23. Martin Luther, *Luther's Works, Volume 26 (Lectures on Galatians Chapters 1–4)* (Concordia Publishing House, 1963), 10.

24. This is the same teacher described in the Introduction.

Chapter 13

1. Martin H. Scharlemann, "Scriptural Concepts of the Church and State," in *Church and State Under God*, Concordia Heritage Series (Concordia Publishing House, 1985), 23.

2. Kurt Aland et al., *The Greek New Testament*, 3rd Edition (Corrected) (Federal Republic of Germany: United Bible Societies, 1983), 660.

3. Aland et al., 660.

4. R. C. H. Lenski, *The Interpretation of St. Paul's Epistles to the Galatians to the Ephesians and to the Philippians* (Augsburg Publishing House, 1962), 273.

5. See the section entitled "Parishioner Disengagement" and the commentary concerning 1 Timothy 2:1–6.

6. See the section entitled "Engagement in the Public Square as Mission."

7. R. C. H. Lenski, *The Interpretation of St. Paul's First and Second Epistles to the Corinthians* (Augsburg Publishing House, 1963), 1018.

8. Philip Edgcumbe Hughes, *Paul's Second Epistle to the Corinthians* (Wm. B. Eerdmans Publishing Co., 1962), 186.

9. Aland et al., *The Greek New Testament*, 630.

10. This thesis insists that pastors must work to persuade their parishioners in order that they would labor to persuade in the public square.

11. Lenski, *The Interpretation of St. Paul's First and Second Epistles to the Corinthians*, 1018.

12. Hughes, *Paul's Second Epistle to the Corinthians*, 210.

13. David E. Garland, *2 Corinthians: An Exegetical and Theological Exposition of Holy Scripture*, vol. 29, The New American Commentary, ed. E. Ray Clendenen (Broadman & Holman Publishers, 2001), 295.

14. Craig L. Blomberg, *Matthew: An Exegetical and Theological Exposition of Holy Scripture*, vol. 22, The New American Commentary ed. David S. Dockery (Broadman & Holman Publishers, 1992), 330.

15. Blomberg, 22:331.

16. Henry Fairfield Burton, "The Worship of Roman Emperors," *The Biblical World* 40, no. 2 (August 1912): 83.

17. Michael Morrison, "Romans 13 and Christian Submission to Civil Authority," accessed April 6, 2023, https://learn.gcs.edu/mod/page/view.php?id=4267.

18. Francis A. Schaeffer, *A Christian Manifesto* (Crossway Books, 1981), 90–91.

19. C. K. Barrett, *The Epistle to Romans* (Hendrickson Publishers, Inc., 1991), 248.

20. Exodus 1:15–21; Joshua 2; 1 Kings 18:4; Psalm 94:20; Isaiah 10:1–2; Jeremiah 22:13; Daniel 3:1–12, 6:4–12; Matthew 2; Revelation 13:14; and the like.

21. James Strong, *The Exhaustive Concordance of the Bible*, Electronic Edition (Woodside Bible Fellowship, 1996), G1783.

22. Gerhard Friedrich, ed., *Theological Dictionary of the New Testament*, vol. 8 (Eerdmans, 1976), 244.

23. Jan Willem Henten, "Cleopatra in Josephus: From Herod's Rival to the Wise Ruler's Opposite," in *The Wisdom of Egypt: Jewish, Early Christian, and Gnostic Essays in Honour of Gerard P. Luttikhuizen*, vol. 59, Ancient Judaism and Early Christianity (Brill Publishers, 2005), 115–16, https://doi.org/10.1163/9789047407676_008.

24. "Rights of Roman Citizens," accessed April 7, 2023, http://www.tribunesandtriumphs.org/roman-life/rights-of-roman-citizens.htm. Paul's actions are tantamount to a first-century lawsuit.

25. "Calvin Coolidge," Oxford Reference, accessed May 29, 2025, https://www.oxfordreference.com/display/10.1093/acref/9780191826719.001.0001/q-oro-ed4-00003260.

26. Christopher I. Thoma, "Departments: Commonplaces," *Touchstone: A Journal of Mere Christianity* 36, no. 5 (October 2023): 8.

Chapter 14

1. John Witte Jr., "Facts and Fictions About the History of Separation of Church and State," *Journal of Church and State* 48, no. 1 (Winter 2006): 28, https://doi.org/10.1093/jcs/48.1.15.

2. Witte, 29.

3. Witte, 30.

4. Witte, 31–32.

5. Witte, 32.

6. Witte, 33.

7. Witte, 33–34.

8. Witte, 34.

9. Witte, 40.

10. Witte, 43.

11. David Sehat, *The Myth of American Religious Freedom* (Oxford University Press, 2015), 298–99.

12. András Sajó, "Preliminaries to a Concept of Constitutional Secularism," *International Journal of Constitutional Law* 6, no. 3–4 (July 2008): 615.

13. Sajó, 609.

14. Sajó, 617.

15. Sajó, 617.

16. John R. Vile and Michael P. Bobic, "Accommodationism and Religion," The First Amendment Encyclopedia: Presented by the John Seigenthaler Chair of Excellence in First Amendment Studies, 2017, August 12, 2023, https://www.mtsu.edu/first-amendment/article/825/accommodationism-and-religion.

17. Abraham Kuyper, *Abraham Kuyper: A Centennial Reader* (Wm. B. Eerdmans Publishing, 1998), 468.

18. Witte, "Facts and Fictions," 23. Here, Witte notes that Luther's Two Kingdoms theology is a returning "to a variation on Augustine's two-cities theory," which, on page 18, he sees iterated in Augustine's work *City of God*. There, "Augustine contrasted the City of God with the City of Man." The City of God dealt with salvation and the Christian life. The City of Man "consisted of . . . the political and social institutions that God had commanded to maintain a modicum of order and peace."

19. Robert S. Alley, *James Madison on Religious Liberty* (Prometheus Books, 1985), 82.

20. Martin Luther, *Christians and Government*, trans. Holger Sonntag (Lutheran Press, 2024), 35. Luther argued that "Christians do not need" a Christianized earthly government by virtue of their residence in the kingdom of Christ.

21. Martin Luther, *On Christian Liberty*, trans. W. A. Lambert and Harold J. Grimm (Fortress Press, 2003), 7–9, 54–55. Consider this resource for a fuller understanding of Luther's perspective on Christian liberty.

22. James M. Stayer, *Martin Luther, German Saviour: German Evangelical Theological Factions and the Interpretation of Luther, 1917–1933* (McGill-Queen's University Press, 2000), 88–90.

23. Robert P. Ericksen, *Theologians Under Hitler: Gerhard Kittel, Paul Altaus, and Emanuel Hirsch* (Yale University Press, 1985), 79–81.

24. Eric Metaxas, *Bonhoeffer: Pastor, Martyr, Prophet, Spy* (Thomas Nelson, 2010), 150–53.

25. Ericksen, *Theologians Under Hitler*, 79–81.

26. Metaxas, *Bonhoeffer*, 150–53.

27. Christopher J. Probst, *Demonizing the Jews: Luther and the Protestant Church in Nazi Germany* (Indiana University Press, 2012), 45–47.

28. Dietrich Bonhoeffer, *Ethics*, ed. Clifford J. Green, trans. Reinhard Krauss, Charles C. West, and Douglas W. Stott (Fortress Press, 2012), 21–23, 252–54.

29. Stayer, *Martin Luther, German Saviour*, 88–90.

30. Ericksen, *Theologians Under Hitler*, 85–87.

31. Probst, *Demonizing the Jews*, 60–62.

32. Richard Steigmann-Gall, *The Holy Reich: Nazi Conceptions of Christianity, 1919–1945* (Cambridge University Press, 2003), 33–35.

33. Richard Winston and Clara Winston, trans., *Inside the Third Reich: Memoirs* (Macmillan, 1970), 96.

34. Steigmann-Gall, *The Holy Reich*, 91–93.

Chapter 15

1. "2024 Republican Party Platform | The American Presidency Project," accessed May 29, 2025, https://www.presidency.ucsb.edu/documents/2024-republican-party-platform.

2. The Democratic Platform, "Party Platform," *Democrats* (blog), accessed May 29, 2025, https://democrats.org/where-we-stand/party-platform/.

3. David Boaz, *Libertarianism: A Primer* (Free Press, 1997), 22–30.

4. Wayne Grudem, *Politics—According to the Bible: A Comprehensive Resource for Understanding Modern Political Issues in Light of Scripture* (Zondervan, 2010), 49–60.

5. George Herbert, *The Complete English Poems*, ed. John Tobin (Penguin Classics, 2004), 182.

6. Jack Phillips and Barronelle Stutzman are ready examples.

7. Jennifer Bauwens, "Protecting the Vulnerable: A Call to Uphold Ethical Standards in Treating Gender Confusion," FRC, June 22, 2021, https://www.frc.org/issuebrief/protecting-the-vulnerable-a-call-to-uphold-ethical-standards-in-treating-gender-confusion.

8. Michigan Catholic Conference, "Protect Life—Vote NO on Proposal 3 | Michigan Catholic Conference," September 21, 2022, https://www.micatholic.org/advocacy/news-room/focus/2022/protect-life-vote-no-on-proposal-3/.

9. Alice Miranda Ollstein, "Republicans Start Sticking to the Script on Abortion," *Politico*, October 17, 2024, https://www.politico.com/newsletters/inside-congress/2024/10/17/republicans-start-sticking-to-the-script-on-abortion-00184221.

10. Michael J. New, "Despite Media Spin, New Gallup Poll Shows Gain in pro-Life Sentiment," *Live Action News* (blog), June 16, 2023, https://www.liveaction.org/news/media-spin-gallup-gain-pro-life-sentiment/.

11. Brooke Singman, "RNC Announces 'Pride Coalition,' Partnership with Log Cabin Republicans Ahead of Midterms," Fox News, November

8, 2021, https://www.foxnews.com/politics/rnc-announces-pride-coalition-partnership-with-log-cabin-republicans-ahead-of-midterms; "About Log Cabin Republicans," *Log Cabin Republicans* (blog), accessed May 29, 2025, https://logcabin.org/about-us/.

12. Liam Beran, "Why the GOP Removed Anti-Gay Language from Its Platform," August 1, 2024, https://www.thenation.com/article/politics/republican-convention-2024-lgbtq-party-platform/.

13. KFUO Radio, "Friends For Life — LCMS Life, Health and Family Ministries: S6Ep5. Protecting the Christian Conscience in the Civic Realm | Rev. Dr. Christopher Thoma," *KFUO Radio* (blog), October 4, 2024, https://www.kfuo.org/2024/10/04/friends-for-life-s6ep5-protecting-the-christian-conscience-in-the-civic-realm-rev-dr-christopher-thoma/.

14. Matthew Harrison, "Baptized for This Moment," *The Lutheran Witness* (blog), April 8, 2013, https://witness.lcms.org/2013/baptized-for-this-moment-4-2013/.

15. G. K. Chesterton, *Orthodoxy* (Moody Publishers, 2009), 25–27.

16. Jean Piaget, *The Origins of Intelligence in Children*, trans. Margaret Cook (International Universities Press, 1952), 7–12.

Chapter 16

1. Elliot Aronson, *Social Psychology*, 10th ed. (Pearson, 2020). The entirety of Aronson's sixth chapter, "The Need to Justify Our Actions," is a helpful primer concerning familiarity bias and resistance to new roles in social groups.

2. Dietrich Bonhoeffer, *The Cost of Discipleship* (Macmillan, 1963), 110–11.

3. Angus J. L. Menuge, *Christ and Culture in Dialogue: Constructive Themes and Practical Applications*, ed. William R. Cario, Alberto L. Garcia, and Dale E. Griffin (Concordia Publishing House, 1999), 38–43.

4. Bonhoeffer, *The Cost of Discipleship*, 61–62.

5. Bonhoeffer, 98.

Chapter 17

1. Thomas Erikson, *Surrounded by Liars: How to Stop Half-Truths, Deception, and Gaslighting from Ruining Your Life* (St. Martin's Publishing Group, 2024). An excellent read relative to discerning and dealing with deception.

2. Ted Griffith, *Theater of Lies: Misinformation Divides Us—With Purpose. How to Protect Ourselves, & Why We Must* (FriesenPress, 2024), 37.

3. Mark Twain, *Pudd'nhead Wilson*, American Artists Edition, vol. 3 (Harper and Brothers, 1922), 51.

4. Jon Brown, "Son of Jailed Canadian Pastor Faces Potential Fines, Prison for Preaching Outside Kids' Drag Queen Story Time," Fox News, April

18, 2023, https://www.foxnews.com/world/pawlowski-son-jailed-canadian-pastor-faces-potential-fines-prison-preaching-outside-kids-drag-queen-story-time.

5. "An After School Satan Club Could Be Coming to Your Kid's Elementary School," *The Washington Post,* July 30, 2016, https://www.washingtonpost.com/local/education/an-after-school-satan-club-could-be-coming-to-your-kids-elementary-school/2016/07/30/63f485e6-5427-11e6-88eb-7dda4e2f2aec_story.html; Larry D. Curtis, "After School Satan Club Holds Utah Open House at Vista Elementary," January 12, 2017, https://kutv.com/news/local/after-school-satan-club-holds-utah-open-house-vista-elementary; "Satanic Temple Brings 'After School Satan Club' to Portland School," Fox News, September 27, 2016, https://www.foxnews.com/us/satanic-temple-brings-after-school-satan-club-to-portland-school.

6. Roseanne Colletti, "Elementary Kids Get 'Special Surprise' Drag Performance at School Talent Show," NBC New York, June 2, 2017, https://www.nbcnewyork.com/news/local/nyc-elementary-kids-get-surprise-drag-queen-performance-talent-show/1700057/.

7. Zachary Rogers, "'A Drag Queen for Every School': Michigan AG Reportedly Dismisses Concerns over Kids, Drag," June 16, 2022, https://wwmt.com/news/local/drag-queens-should-be-in-every-school-michigan-ag-says-at-conference-report-claims-attorney-general-dana-nessel-pride-trans-transgender-students-kids-children; Laura Gibbons, "Dana Nessel Jokingly Calls for 'Drag Queen for Every School.' GOP Not Laughing," Bridge Michigan, June 15, 2022, https://www.bridgemi.com/michigan-government/nessel-jokingly-calls-drag-queen-every-school-gop-not-laughing.

8. Thomas C. Oden, ed., *Mark*, vol. New Testament II, Ancient Christian Commentary on Scripture (Routledge, 1998), 226.

Chapter 18

1. "German Resistance Memorial Center—Biographie," accessed May 29, 2025, https://www.gdw-berlin.de/en/recess/biographies/index_of_persons/biographie/view-bio/busso-thoma/?no_cache=1.

2. Peter Hoffman, *The History of the German Resistance, 1933–1945*, 3rd ed. (McGill-Queen's University Press, 1996), 389–400.

3. Stephanie Palek, "Operation Valkyrie 1944," Text, April 27, 2015, https://www.lib.cam.ac.uk/collections/departments/germanic-collections/about-collections/spotlight-archive/operation-valkyrie.

4. "German Resistance Memorial Center—Biographie."

5. "Bendlerblock in Berlin: German Resistance Memorial Today," *Maksym Chorny's Personal Blog on WWII* (blog), June 18, 2022, https://war-documentary.info/bendlerblock-memorial-in-berlin-july-20-1944/.

6. "Assault and Coup of July 20th, 1944," TracesOfWar.Com, accessed May 29, 2025, https://www.tracesofwar.com/articles/4729/Assault-and-coup-of-July-20th-1944.htm.

Conclusion

1. Flavius Josephus, *The Antiquities of the Jews*, trans. William Whiston (Hendrickson Publishers, 1987), 480.

2. Origen, *Contra Celsum*, trans. Henry Chadwick (Cambridge University Press, 1953), 94. Origen cites the pagan philosopher, Celsus, who wrote a hostile critique of Christianity around AD 175–180. His work, *The True Word*, is preserved in Origen's rebuttal. Celsus claims the resurrection was a fabrication, even suggesting the disciples stole the body. Ironically, this preserves evidence of early counterarguments to the resurrection, which means Christians were defending the resurrection against accusations of theft and fabrication from the very beginning.

3. Pliny the Younger, *The Letters of the Younger Pliny*, trans. Betty Radice (Penguin Books, 1969), 294–96. Pliny describes early Christians as gathering "on a fixed day" (Sunday) to sing hymns "to Christ as to a god" and to live moral lives. The implications suggest a risen and worshiped Christ, not a memorable, but nevertheless dead, teacher.

4. Tacitus, *The Annals of Imperial Rome*, trans. Michael Grant (Penguin Books, 1956), 365.

5. Clement of Rome, *The First Epistle of Clement to the Corinthians* in *The Apostolic Fathers*, ed. and trans. J. B. Lightfoot (Baker Book House, 1984), 58.

6. Philip Schaff, *History of the Christian Church, Volume III: Nicene and Post-Nicene Christianity. A.D. 311–600* (Wm. B. Eerdmans Publishing Co., 1995), 39–59.

7. "Church Fathers: Ecclesiastical History, Book III (Theodoret)," accessed May 30, 2025, https://www.newadvent.org/fathers/27023.htm.

8. Rowan Williams, *Why Study the Past?: The Quest for the Historical Church* (Wm. B. Eerdmans Publishing Co., 2018), 20.

Glossary of Terms

1. Alpheus Thomas Mason and Donald Grier Stephenson Jr., *American Constitutional Law: Introductory Essays and Selected Cases*, 16th edition (Pearson, 2011), 530–31.

2. Christopher Pappas, "The Adult Learning Theory: Andragogy of Malcolm Knowles," eLearning Industry, October 2, 2025, https://elearningindustry.com/the-adult-learning-theory-andragogy-of-malcolm-knowles.

3. Nicole Dudenhoefer, "Is Cancel Culture Effective? How Public Shaming Has Changed," *Pegasus Magazine*, Fall 2020, https://www.ucf.edu/pegasus/is-cancel-culture-effective/.

4. "Separation of Church and State," LII / Legal Information Institute, accessed March 29, 2023, https://www.law.cornell.edu/wex/separation_of_church_and_state.

5. Jason G. Goldman, "What Is Classical Conditioning? (And Why Does It Matter?)," Scientific American Blog Network, January 11, 2012, https://blogs.scientificamerican.com/thoughtful-animal/what-is-classical-conditioning-and-why-does-it-matter/.

6. Zawn Villines, "Cognitive Dissonance: Definition, Effects, and Examples," January 15, 2024, https://www.medicalnewstoday.com/articles/326738.

7. Leon Festinger, *A Theory of Cognitive Dissonance* (Stanford University Press, 1962), 3–4.

8. Wil Waluchow and Dimitrios Kyritsis, "Constitutionalism," in *The Stanford Encyclopedia of Philosophy*, ed. Edward N. Zalta, Summer 2022 (Metaphysics Research Lab, Stanford University, 2022), https://plato.stanford.edu/archives/sum2022/entries/constitutionalism/.

9. Richard Delgado and Jean Stefancic, *Critical Race Theory*, 3rd edition (NYU Press, 2017), 3.

10. Alfred Louis Kroeber and Clyde Kluckhohn, *Culture: A Critical Review of Concepts and Definitions* (Kraus Reprint Company, 1978), 35.

11. Erwin L. Lueker, ed., *Lutheran Cyclopedia: A Concise In-Home Reference for the Christian Family* (Concordia Publishing House, 1975), 227.

12. Natasha Crain, "Disagreement Fatigue and 2020: How the Events of the Year Will Shape Christian Interactions in 2021 and Beyond," December 29, 2020, https://natashacrain.com/disagreement-fatigue-and-2020-how-the-events-of-the-year-will-shape-christian-interactions-in-2021-and-beyond/.

13. Keri Ladner, "The Quiet Rise of Christian Dominionism," *The Christian Century*, 2022, 48–50.

14. "Establishment Clause," LII / Legal Information Institute, accessed March 30, 2023, https://www.law.cornell.edu/wex/establishment_clause.

15. "Free Exercise of Religion," Justia Law, accessed March 30, 2023, https://law.justia.com/constitution/us/amendment-01/03-free-exercise-of-religion.html.

16. O. C. Edwards, Jr., *Elements of Homiletic: A Method for Preparing to Preach* (Pueblo Publishing Company, 1982), 1–16.

17. John R. Vile, "Johnson Amendment," accessed March 30, 2023, https://www.mtsu.edu/first-amendment/article/1744/johnson-amendment.

18. Christopher I. Thoma, "Johnson Amendment Summary," accessed March 30, 2023, https://www.facebook.com/RevChristopherThoma/posts/151839393222108.

19. Lueker, *Lutheran Cyclopedia*, 567–68.

20. Philip M. Anderson, *Pedagogy Primer* (Peter Lang, 2009), 41.

21. James Mildred, "What Is the 'Public Square'?," CARE, April 12, 2022, https://care.org.uk/news/2022/04/what-is-the-public-square.

22. Paul D. Bush, "'Radical Individualism' vs. Institutionalism, II: Philosophical Dualisms as Apologetic Constructs Based on Obsolete Psychological Preconceptions," *The American Journal of Economics and Sociology* 40, no. 3 (1981): 292–94.

23. Jonathan Haidt, *The Righteous Mind: Why Good People Are Divided by Politics and Religion* (Vintage Books, 2013), 116, 228–29.

24. Andrew Copson, *Secularism: Politics, Religion, and Freedom* (Oxford University Press, 2017), 2–6.

25. "Accommodationist and Separationist Theories of the Establishment Clause: Constitution Annotated, Library of Congress," accessed March 30, 2023, https://constitution.congress.gov/browse/essay/amdt1-3-2/ALDE_00013072/.

26. W. Bradford Littlejohn, *The Two Kingdoms: A Guide for the Perplexed* (The Davenant Press, 2017), 8.

27. Owen Strachan, *Christianity and Wokeness: How the Social Justice Movement Is Hijacking the Gospel—and the Way to Stop It* (Salem Books, 2021), 8.

28. James Swanson, "Dictionary of Biblical Languages with Semantic Domains: Greek (New Testament)" (Logos Research Systems, Inc., 1997), 3180: 3–4.